An Infuriating
American

MUSE BOOKS
The Iowa Series in Creativity and Writing
Robert D. Richardson, series editor

An Infuriating American

The Incendiary Arts of
H. L. Mencken

by Hal Crowther

University of Iowa Press | Iowa City

University of Iowa Press, Iowa City 52242
Copyright © 2014 by the University of Iowa Press
www.uiowapress.org
Printed in the United States of America
Design by Sara T. Sauers

The University of Iowa Press is a member of Green Press
Initiative and is committed to preserving natural resources.

Printed on acid-free paper

Library of Congress Cataloging-in-Publication Data
Crowther, Hal.
An infuriating American: the incendiary arts of
H. L. Mencken / by Hal Crowther.
    pages   cm
Includes bibliographical references and index.
ISBN 978-1-60938-281-0 (pbk)
1. Mencken, H. L. (Henry Louis), 1880–1956. 2. Authors,
American—20th century—Biography. 3. Journalists—
United States—Biography. 4. Editors—United States—
Biography.   I. Title.
PS3525.E43Z546 2014
818'.5209—dc23
[B]   2014010200

For Jeffrey, gentleman, scholar—brother

Contents

An Infuriating American

A Disarming Introduction to an Alarming American

Education in the truest sense— education directed toward awakening a capacity to differentiate between fact and appearance— always will be a more or less furtive and illicit thing, for its chief purpose is the controversion and destruction of the very ideas that the majority of men—and particularly the majority of official and powerful men—regard as incontrovertibly true. To the extent that I am genuinely educated, I am suspicious of all the things that the average citizen believes and the average pedagogue teaches. Progress consists entirely of attacking and disposing of these ordinary beliefs. —H. L. Mencken, *The Smart Set*, March 1921

MENCKEN. Dead for nearly 60 years, with a legacy of some 10 million recorded words by his own reckoning, a body of work that by any reckoning must be as large as any man of letters ever produced in English, Latin, Greek, or Farsi. Somehow the man grew, posthumously, as more of his unpublished work became available, attracted commentary and memoir, inspired new biographers, new scholarship—new websites, as the technophobe Mencken would have been appalled to comprehend. A public life that ended in 1948, a national and international influence that ended a decade earlier, and still Mencken is almost too big to approach with any confidence. Setting yourself to write about him, you feel like an old farmer with his old mule, at sunrise of a long, hot day, looking out over 50 acres that ought to be plowed before sundown. Give me strength, Lord, and where do I begin?

The literary territory marked "HLM" on our maps is a wilderness of pitfalls, switchbacks, and quicksand crisscrossed by a thousand trails, many of them blazed by writers who lost their way and left no coherent account of their adventures. Is it important, is it necessary, to go there? There are American writers of greater depth, and dedicated journalists with exemplary careers of clear thinking and public service, who have been ignored by scholars and biographers, virtually buried in potter's fields by posterity. There are recognized arbiters of literary achievement and philosophical resonance who consign Mencken to the second or third rank, a kind of poetic justice for this hanging judge of a critic whose harsh custom was to dismiss most of his contemporaries as "third-rate" talent or worse. The famous Algonquin Round Table of literary wits and bon vivants, whose collective fame has endured almost as well as his own, he swept aside in a magisterial wave of disrespect as "literati of the third, fourth and fifth rate."

But Mencken, who flayed academics mercilessly all his life and compared them to things invertebrate and inanimate, did not anticipate much posthumous support from PhDs. To those of us who called ourselves working journalists—I recorded my first professional byline just five years after his death—and now watch numbly as we're replaced by what Mencken might call "a rancid miscellany" of entertainers, gossips, cover models, flacks, Internet narcissists, propagandists, and headline readers, Mencken's long reign on a media throne of his own creation seems as grand and legendary as the heyday of Giotto must seem to the planet's last fresco artists. Those were the days, or so we all imagine. Has any journalist since been hailed as "the civilized consciousness of America," a crown of laurels bestowed on Mencken by no less a figure than Edmund Wilson?

Wilson, a critic and public intellectual with a Princeton

pedigree, is now respected as a more highbrow, possibly more reliable authority on the letters and politics of the era he shared with Mencken. But he never failed to honor his debt to the older man, whom he ranked as "without question, since Poe, our greatest practicing literary journalist." Wilson's outsized regard for Mencken was echoed by other heavyweight critics of the day, notably Walter Lippmann and Joseph Wood Krutch—also holders of diplomas from the Ivy League that HLM loved to ridicule. Lippmann, reviewing *Notes on Democracy* in 1926, virtually deified its author as "the most powerful personal influence on this whole generation of educated people." Krutch, writing Mencken's obituary for the *Nation* in 1956, went even further, predicting an eventual consensus that "Mencken's was the best prose written in America during the 20th century."

These learned gentlemen were taken very seriously, by themselves among others, and did not dispense superlatives lightly. The fact that his peers paid such homage to Mencken, with all his quirks, is one measure of his pervasive influence in this country at the time they were in college. (My grandfather, who graduated from college in 1912, was an initiate who introduced me to Mencken when I was barely in high school.) Besides their Ivy pedigrees, they fell into several of the categories of Americans that Mencken routinely abused. Lippmann was a Jew, Krutch was a Southerner *and* a PhD, and Wilson flirted with communism in his youth and defended Stalin as late as 1935. None of them were in line with Mencken's politics. Yet in the Twenties they were among his staunchest allies.

It's a fair question whether any journalist before or since has been so popular with his peers—his competitors, if you will. It has been suggested, of course, that they lived in terror of offending him, like nearly everyone else. But conservatives of our current century, who attempt to adopt Mencken as a soul father for his critiques of democracy and the New Deal, are stalled in confusion when they discover that so many of Mencken's friends and associates were leftists, and even Marxists like Theodore Dreiser and Philip Goodman. In these days of mindless, hostile polarization, we forget that in their day even fewer people were equipped to debate serious ideas, and that no matter how contentiously they disagreed they had more in common with each other than with all the others, the lumpen masses with no ideas at all.

"Conservative" meant something quite different then, too. Certainly Mencken was a conservative by many measures, and died conspicuously to the right of the intellectual mainstream. But it's a grievous insult and injustice to imagine him watching Fox News, or celebrating the wisdom of Rush Limbaugh and Ayn Rand. Or to conflate him with the oxygen-starved brains that conceived the Tea Party—sadly, the same tribe of benighted hominids he expelled from the human race in his dispatches on the Scopes "Monkey Trial" in 1925. Sorrow of sorrows, one of them who rejects evolution, embryology, and the Big Bang theory as "lies straight from the pit of Hell" was recently a "conservative" candidate for a US Senate seat in Georgia. Human progress was one of the myths to which Mencken did not subscribe. By the standards of his time, he was actually a radical. When you begin by tossing out God and country, as he did exuberantly, there's not much left in the conservative cupboard except family, and he had his doubts about that, too.

In the USA of today, where journalists rank even lower than congressmen in polls of the public's trust and respect, the legend of a man with a typewriter hailed as "the civilized consciousness of America" sounds like a senile reporter's daydream. The *Washington Post* and the *Boston Globe* have been sold for peanuts, for 10 cents on the dollar compared to their value 20 years ago, and a Pulitzer Prize plus $4.75 will still get you a double latte at Starbucks. Popular websites masquerading as news media now admit that traffic often trumps the truth—if an apocryphal story attracts enough revenue-producing "hits," they embrace it without fact checks or apologies. In Mexico and other failed states, people shoot reporters like rats. That Mencken once ruled educated opinion much the way Bismarck ruled Germany, that he was a Pied Piper trailed by legions of undergraduates and aspiring savants, that he was courted by movie stars and hailed in Europe as the reigning prince of the press—how can we imagine these things in our blasted cultural landscape where "celebrity journalism" is not recognized as an oxymoron?

What bewilders us now, what Mencken achieved that no scribe has approached since or will approach again, was his sheer *Size*—the pie was so much smaller then, and his slice was so huge. To the lowly, marginalized class of newsrats who've inherited what's left of the Fourth Estate, the reign of Mencken shines in the rearview mirror like some Golden Age. It's little wonder that writers continue to exhume him, to poke at his remains and marvel at the long shadow he once cast across America. Even more remarkable than his impact was his strange doubleness, the veil of contradiction that bars the way to the elusive identity of Henry Louis Mencken. If his peers judged him eloquent and dangerous, his victims and inferiors judged him subhuman. A survey by biographer Terry Teachout (*The Skeptic*, 2002) revealed that Mencken was the subject of 500 newspaper editorials in the year 1926 alone, and that at least 400 were negative. He saved them all in a scrapbook and published the worst of them in *Menckeniana: A Schimpflexicon*. A sample: "Mencken, with his filthy verbal hemorrhages, is so low down in the moral scale, so damnably dirty, so vile and degenerate, that when his time comes to die it will take a special dispensation from Heaven to get him into the bottom-most pit of hell."

An editorial in the *Palm Beach News* named Mencken "the most universally hated man in the United States." He gloried in such stuff, of course, and in the incorrigible stupidity of the yahoos who produced it. But people who knew him well and spent years in his close company also contradict each other when they remember Mencken, so often that his portrait is perpetually blurred. Fred Hobson, one of Mencken's most thorough and convincing biographers, titles one chapter (*Mencken: A Life*, 1994) "A Loneliness at the Core." Drawing mainly from Mencken's own correspondence and conversations, Hobson makes a case for recurring depression and spells of despair. But Sara Mayfield, Sara Haardt Mencken's closest friend and an intimate of the Menckens for decades, writes in her memoir *The Constant Circle* (1968) that "no author I've ever known was less a lonely man than Mencken." She remembers a man "gregarious and friendly by nature," an extrovert "popular both with men and women, always in demand among his numerous friends, constantly entertaining and being entertained." Hamilton Owens, his colleague at the *Sunpapers*, concurred: "Never was a man more gregarious, never one who strove more generously to keep his friendships green."

They're speaking of the same man who wrote, in *Autobiographical Notes* (1941), "I get little pleasure out of meeting people, and avoid it as much as possible." George Jean Nathan, Mencken's closest professional associate through their years at *The Smart Set* and *The American Mercury*, left a marvelous profile of his partner, one that's built entirely from the bricks of paradox. "He writes vehemently against quack doctors and has tried ten of them in an attempt to get rid of his hay fever,"

Nathan recalls. "He insists that he likes only the company of middle-aged women, and associates solely with young ones. . . . He is an exponent of the 'Be hard' doctrine, is in favor of killing off the weak, and sends milk twice a month to the starving babies of the war-ridden European countries." And so forth. Apparently Mencken was such a master of disguise that his biographers have failed to reach a consensus on the way he dressed. One English journalist wrote that he dressed "like the owner of a country hardware store" or "on ceremonial occasions . . . like a plumber got up for church." Yet one of the contradictions on Nathan's list is this: "He scorns society, but has his evening clothes made by one of the best and most expensive of Fifth Avenue tailors."

Dressed to the nines, was Mencken Maurice Chevalier or Jed Clampett? In this case we should probably trust Nathan, a notorious dandy who knew a nice jacket when he saw one. And perhaps all Americans look like Jed Clampett to the English. As a rule the private lives and personal eccentricities of writers are a voyeuristic distraction from their work, of little relevance to their literary prestige. If Edmund Wilson was a fat, petulant egoist with a chronic case of satyriasis, he was also a brilliant critic whose ear for language was a public treasure. But in the case of Mencken we have to begin by recognizing that he was a major American celebrity, on a par in his prime with Babe Ruth and Al Jolson. In one of his playful letters to his North Carolina friend Betty Hanes, he complains that the Hearst newspapers persist in linking him to one Hollywood actress after another.

Who was that masked man in the Fifth Avenue tuxedo who looked like a plumber to the Brits? Biographers can't resist the enigma of the private Mencken, in part because his meditations, so copious, shed so little light on his primary motivation—on what he really thought about the work he did so well, and so successfully. The pathology, the primal impulse that animated him and all his fellow men and women of letters, was of course no mystery to Mencken. "An author is simply a man in whom the normal vanity of all men is so vastly exaggerated that he finds it a sheer impossibility to hold it in," he wrote in 1926, in the *Chicago Sunday Tribune* ("On Literary Gents"). "His overpowering impulse is to gyrate before his fellow men, flapping his wings and emitting his defiant yells. This being forbidden by the *polizei* of all civilized countries, he takes it out by putting his yells on paper. Such is the thing called self-expression."

Yet the nature of literary creation—the clockwork of the literary mind—is a subject he prefers to avoid. The most certain thing we know is that Mencken experienced nausea when writing was dissected in what he considered effeminate, highbrow language. This idiom was ponderously employed by Charles Angoff, his onetime editorial assistant and most hostile biographer, who charged in his book (*H. L. Mencken: A Portrait from Memory*, 1956) that Mencken was ignorant of "the process of writing, its spiritual and psychological propulsions, its moral overtones, its esthetic essence." We can almost hear Mencken expectorating, in the general direction of his spittoon. He was a newspaperman, not an assistant professor or a lyric poet. Writing was not a sacrament. He offered his prejudices to America and always insisted that he was indifferent to its response.

"I don't give a damn what any American thinks of me," he once told Theodore Dreiser, and it's worth considering whether any other American writer would have said that, publicly or privately. "I wrote what I wrote because it was in my nature to do so, and for no other reason," he reasserts in the preface to *My Life as Author and Editor*. "As I have often observed, my fundamental satisfaction was indistinguished from the satisfaction a hen enjoys in laying an egg." His disclaimers of indignation or crusading intent cover the entire barnyard. He also said, "My writings, such as they are, have had only one purpose: to attain for H. L. Mencken that feeling of tension relieved and function achieved which a cow enjoys on giving milk."

Naturally it's hard to give full credit to these pleadings of utter (udder?) disinterest, these tranquil metaphors from the henhouse and the dairy barn, from this writer who participated so vehemently in the national discourse that he succeeded, as many have argued, in altering it permanently. As a journalist who, like Mencken, has been a lifelong retailer of personal opinion, I know that any such claims of detachment and indifference would amount to a transparent fraud on my part. Was Mencken a fraud, Mencken who fancied himself above all as the great fraud-slayer? Not a conscious fraud, I think. But like many other people, perhaps most of them, he was imperfect at introspection. He had an idea of himself that was at odds with some of the things that actually made him tick, and it's one of the things that makes him so intriguing.

Hobson's research, digging a little deeper into the man Mencken at work, uncovered some thoughts that he did not have in common with cows and chickens. "The writing profession is reeking with this loneliness, this melancholy," he was once moved to complain, in 1928. "All our lives we spend in discoursing with ourselves.... The loneliest people in the world we writers are." "What a life!" he wrote to his friend, the opera singer Gretchen Hood. "I wish I had studied drumming and taken to the road. It is a dreadful thing to sit in a room alone."

Where, there, is the contented cow, the happy warrior who launched his rockets with no thought where they might fall? It's Hobson's contention that some of Mencken's prodigious energy—no one in any profession worked harder—was expended in running from personal demons, and that the cheerful indifference, the insistence that it was all a bracing game, was something of a pose. This biographer goes so far as to claim that "work, for Mencken, was a means of avoiding the abyss, of keeping the emptiness at bay."

There's a suspicion, also, that Mencken's rule against righteous indignation was suspended on occasion. Friends recalled that he returned from the Scopes trial stunned, even frightened by the ignorance and passion of the fundamentalists he encountered in Tennessee. "I set out laughing and returned quivering," he related. William Jennings Bryan died shortly after the trial, perhaps terminally exhausted by the heat and HLM's vicious ridicule of his role in the proceedings. Mencken boasted to his friends, "We killed the son-of-a-bitch." From his famously cruel obituary for Bryan, "In Memoriam: W. J. B.," he deleted a last sentence, a prophetic one that conveys neither amusement nor detachment: "The job before democracy is to get rid of such canaille. If it fails, they will devour it." Attention, twenty-first-century Americans: If H. L. Mencken sounded just one indispensable warning to posterity, this must be the one.

"Canaille," one of those five-dollar words so dear to Mencken, means the rabble, the riffraff, the illiterate and unwashed. It's a French word, a term of special contempt derived from an Italian word that means "cane-dogs." In spite of Mencken's pseudo-populist, city-desk disdain for plutocrats, Harvard dons, and Boston Brahmins, he was an incurable elitist who discerned nothing of value, and much to fear, in the all-too-common man. It's another Mencken paradox, one among so many, but it's a key one when we try to grasp his political philosophy. In America he saw himself as a minority of one, a single civilized citizen struggling to free himself of the smug bourgeoisie on the one hand and the great lowing herds of unsalvageable morons on the other.

Trying to understand Mencken is a serious commitment, like trying to understand the Unified Theory. We enter, forewarned, this vast labyrinth of paradox. Understanding Mencken's success is much easier. His inimitably belligerent style and droll pessimism owed nothing to any previous American writer except Mark Twain, to whom he was devoted. "In all he writes there is a crackle of blue sparks like those one sees in a dynamo house amongst revolving masses of metal that give you a sense of enormous hidden power," wrote the novelist Joseph Conrad. Mencken at 30, when he began to throw off the sparks that everyone noticed, was an original shining among drab imitations, a tiger released among overweight antelopes. His timing was fortunate. Thanks to general prosperity, more of the children of the middle class were attending elite institutions and encountering the liberal arts. The stale wisdom of parents and preachers no longer hemmed them in, and H. L. Mencken was a guru who illuminated the high road to skepticism and freedom.

Any individual who has such impregnable confidence in his own opinion, and expresses it with such force, tends to undermine the confidence of anyone whose opinion differs. When I read that Mencken scoffed at Melville and Joyce, and belittled Eliot, my natural response is to dismiss him as a tin-eared philistine. But Mencken would contend—or just sneer—that I contracted my respect for these "classics" in a classroom, from scholars who had studied them with older scholars, in a long conga line of scholars. He would be right, and force me to reconsider what I thought and who taught me to think that way. We are all—including Mencken—the products of a certain set of connections and circumstances, and how much original thinking has gone into our aesthetic responses is always a matter for debate. If we're honest we're vulnerable, and Mencken's certainty will unsettle and impress us. "He calls you a swine, and an imbecile," marveled Walter Lippmann, "and he increases your will to live."

To use a coalfields metaphor, extracting literary insights from Mencken's massive oeuvre is more laborious strip-mining than mountaintop removal. The Sage himself left us meager guidance. He told Sara Mayfield that his style was something he was born with, "as natural to him as his breathing" (in Mayfield's words), though he conceded that he had nurtured it with such prose models as Thomas Huxley, Jonathan Swift, Friedrich Nietzsche, Ambrose Bierce, and of course Mark Twain. His rare musings on prose style expand on this genetic, organic model with considerable eloquence. "For the essence of a sound style is that it cannot be reduced to rules—that it is a living and breathing thing, with something of the devilish in it—that it fits its proprietor tightly and yet ever so loosely, as his skin fits him," Mencken writes in *Prejudices, Vol. 5* (1926). "It is, in fact, quite as securely an integral part of him as that skin is. It hardens as his arteries harden. . . . To attempt to teach it is as silly as to set up courses in making love. The man who makes love out of a book is not making love at all. He is simply imitating someone else making love."

In sum, the brain is the gun—Mencken's an imposing weapon, yours noticeably less so—and every writer should choose for himself how to prime and load it, what to read and learn and practice before he takes the field. What Mencken accomplished as a journalist and critic, what made him unique, seems almost inseparable from his problematic and paradoxical personality. He was a great character, a great scandal, and still, arguably, a great man. His defiance of church and state was a huge milestone on the long hard climb toward free speech and respect for the First Amendment, in an adolescent nation where the Second Amendment seems to hold more permanent appeal. His style, laced with hyperbole and unadulterated contempt, has profoundly influenced every form of commentary in this country, up to this day. There are echoes of him in the hydrophobic Westbrook Pegler, who was almost a caricature of Mencken; in the "gonzo" *Rolling Stone* polemics of Hunter Thompson and Matt Taibbi, in the roughshod Lone Star populism of Molly Ivins, even in the bombast of reactionary cretins like Rush Limbaugh.

His voice, filtered through a hundred other voices and shades of opinion, may be with us always. I have not steered a course away from it, myself. I believed from the outset that the best path for a columnist was to be aggressively unaffiliated and so outspoken that venomous objections would come in from readers stationed Left and Right, and like Mencken I felt gratified when the readers obliged me. When the aging Mencken tried to sum himself up, he left us a few fair words to live by. "The two main ideas that run through all my writing are these: I am strongly in favor of liberty, and I hate fraud." Good enough, even if Mencken couldn't always rise to the level of his better angels.

Pick up your hazmat suits and land-mine detectors at the gatehouse here, and follow me, if you're so inclined. A journey into Mencken country is nothing like a walking tour of the Lake District, or of the chateaus along the Loire. For everything we encounter that's inspirational or charming, there's something appalling or incomprehensible. Pretty country, no. But it's never dull, and no one ever returned complaining that it was a waste of time.

Machine Dreams

This Corona, by the way, is a wonder. I bought it in 1916 to go to the war, and have used it ever since. It has traveled nearly 100,000 miles, and I have done at least 10,000,000 words on it, including all my correspondence. It is still as good as new. It has gone from Russia to San Francisco, and from the Orkney Islands to Havana. When it wears out at last I shall present it to the Smithsonian.—Letter from H. L. Mencken to Elizabeth Hanes, Friday 13, 1927

IN ALL the long history of literature, evolving from an oral tradition through centuries of calligraphy and typography to its current shotgun marriage with digital electronics, there was but one lonely century dominated by a machine so suddenly and brutally obsolete that few twenty-first-century college students have ever seen one. Yet nearly everyone old enough to have earned a living or a reputation as a writer remembers a typewriter fondly, even nostalgically. Men and women who once cursed the clumsy carbon paper and the jammed and sticky keys now maintain little shrines for homely old Remingtons and Olivettis, on cleared bookshelves and closet shelves where the retired tools of their trade gather dust in dignified silence.

In the late summer of 2013, a humble obituary in the *Washington Post* paid journalism's last respects to Manson Whitlock, 96, who until a few weeks before his death operated what must have been the last typewriter repair shop in America, near the Yale University campus in New Haven. Whitlock, invariably dressed in a tweed jacket, V-neck sweater, and tie, had been on the job since 1930. He estimated that he'd sold thousands of typewriters in his time—but probably none in the past two decades. Instead of retiring or updating his business, he remained at his post to service the obsolete machines still operated by a few aging customers.

Though the Typewriter Century had ended years earlier, the death of Manson Whitlock was its symbolic "–30–," a final key falling on a last ragged ribbon. The Century's starting point is not as clear. Though prototypes of various kinds have been traced back to the early eighteenth century, the typewriters we recognize were invented and patented in the second half of the nineteenth, several during the American Civil War. Introduced—like computers—as revolutionary tools of commerce, they were embraced with enthusiasm by the writing class, and their literary pedigree was distinguished from the beginning. *Life on the Mississippi* (1883) by Mark Twain, a journalist and typesetter, is believed to be the first important book composed entirely on a typewriter. Henry James dictated most of his novels to a typist—nearly always a female, and in fact "typewriter" was also a pre-feminist term for the women who worked at the keyboards.

Ernest Hemingway, the first Nobel Prize winner who cut his teeth in a newsroom, would set his Royal on top of a bookcase and type all his manuscripts while standing up. William Faulkner created Yoknapatawpha on an Underwood. Jack Kerouac, said to be capable of typing more than 100 words per minute, amphetamine-free, typed *On the Road* on that famous single roll of paper, 120 feet long (single-spaced). Cormac McCarthy, the most prominent American writer who still refuses to go digital, wrote most of his novels on a 1963 pawnshop Olivetti.

By the end of the 1980s the handwriting—typewriting—was on the wall for these humble tools that served our native genius. Within two decades computers and related gadgetry had swallowed the word industry entirely, and typewriters were antiquated curiosities like the pince-nez or the pony cart. But the undeniable quality of the literature they produced—possibly 90 percent of the current American canon was once punched through a typewriter ribbon—is not as critical to their mystique as the atmosphere where they functioned, the Century they helped to create. Writers still argue about the virtues and liabilities of the new technologies; they still dispute whether a typewriter or a laptop is more compatible with creativity and literary achievement, a dispute that will end fairly soon, when the typewriter's last adherents have outlived their memories or gone to their reward. What mattered more, historically, was the personality of the device itself, a clever piece of technology but essentially a democratic hand tool nearly anyone could learn to use.

"Virile" is an unfortunately sexist word for a machine that brought hundreds of thousands of women into the workforce. But it suggests the muscular, blue-collar nature of the typewriter and its milieu. There was a time when building a paragraph sounded like building a fence, and required nearly as much physical effort. Compare it to the silent fountain pens and quills that came before, or the subtle-pressured cybersilence of the electronic "word processors" that came after, and the manual typewriter seems more closely related to the steam drill and the jackhammer. Its heyday was coterminous with the rise of the newspaper industry and the sprawling newsrooms of the great urban dailies. The graying survivors of that newspaper century remember those places, sometimes fondly, as smoky theaters of perpetual melodrama, where a critic trying to explain Antonioni or describe Maggie Smith as Titania could expect to be interrupted hourly by a breaking story, by a fire, murder, rape, or industrial disaster that would raise the newsroom noise level to pain-inducing decibels.

Such a madhouse seemed inimical to any reflective activity, far less prose that aspired to literary art. But the best journalism of the twentieth century is proof of the human animal's uncanny adaptability. Under unbending deadlines, in the midst of bedlam, for a public that neither demanded nor expected it, many of these "ink-stained" and underpaid wretches served the English language with remarkable distinction. And beneath it all—imagine a motion picture with a percussive score that never falls silent—the syncopated symphony of the typewriters, the click of the keys and the crashes and bells of the carriage returns, all with a tempo as varied as the skill and vigor of 100 typists. A sweet sound, to some ears, that will never be heard again on this planet, except in the fitful dreams of old reporters.

Writers bred in the newsroom, from Samuel Clemens forward, heard the voice of a muse radically different from the one who whispered to the cloistered gentry and cultured dons of earlier English literature. They heard a voice considerably louder and less refined in her diction—a muse of the people—and her instrument of expression was no lyre, but 20 pounds of future scrap metal with furious moving parts. It's no coincidence that literary "modernism" and the mechanized newsrooms and pressrooms arrived together. A shorthand definition of modernism was "the reinterpretation of reality." In the golden age of newspapers a rougher, tougher sort of American began to interpret reality, and the new interpretations attracted the most intrepid young talent.

College held no appeal for Clemens or Hemingway, both sons of educated professionals. They learned the writer's trade in places located light years, psychically and socially, from Harvard Yard or the Prufrockian drawing rooms that produced

Henry James and Edith Wharton. The political power and wealth of the Newspaper Age was harvested by bullies like William Randolph Hearst, but its ringing voice, its master of ceremonies—the King Kong of the Keyboard, the Napoleon of the Newsroom—was the singular Henry Louis Mencken. Mencken came equipped with a sturdy, thick-necked physique and a ruddy, truculent countenance, and every inch of him refuted the Romantic image of the wan, tubercular man of letters. We can as easily imagine Wordsworth wielding a chainsaw as Henry Mencken writing with an inkpot and quill. He was the maestro the typewriter was made for, a man for whom words were fired like bullets, not released like butterflies to charm the refined. For many years after his death, that famous Corona remained on display in his home office on Hollins Street. To sit next to it and touch the keys was an experience no less awe-inspiring than a visit to the Smithsonian annex at Dulles Airport to see the *Enola Gay*, the B-29 that dropped the atomic bomb on Hiroshima. With both these silent, mothballed machines there's a lingering sense of shock and smoke, and deadly purpose.

Mencken was another young man, bred to considerable middle-class privilege, who showed little interest in college. He graduated first in his class from Baltimore Polytechnic Institute at the age of 15. According to biographer Fred Hobson he composed his valedictory address on his father's typewriter. He spent the next three years—most unhappily—in the family business, acceding to an autocratic father's wishes and traditional claims on the eldest sons of successful merchants. Only his father's premature death in 1899 released him from Aug. Mencken and Bro., cigar makers. Mencken's immediate response—he sometimes claimed it was the day after the funeral—was to dress himself as he thought a reporter should dress and present his case to the city editor of the Baltimore *Morning Herald.*

To complement copious reading, Mencken had prepared himself for the Fourth Estate by taking correspondence courses in fiction writing and journalism. Naturally nothing in his résumé dazzled the city editor, but he was invited to make himself available for unpaid tryout assignments. His first opportunity, during a February blizzard, resulted in a paragraph about a stolen horse and buggy in Govanstown. But something of the prose style that scorched North America must have been evident even then. It took him several months to win a salary—seven dollars a week—but only a year to take over the City Hall beat and a weekly column on the *Herald*'s editorial page. Still a teenager, Mencken was not only an established knight of the newsroom but well on his way to a career that created an archetype for the American journalist—a new kind of writer, unbuttoned and undaunted, free of the restraints of social class and classrooms.

In a very short time Mencken found precisely the life he wanted, the one he appears to have coveted and envisioned from pre-adolescence. It's not clear that his contempt for higher education dates from those earliest years. Hobson and other biographers agree that his father considered sending him to Johns Hopkins to study law—a lawyer in the family was a tremendous business asset—but there's no evidence that young Henry was tempted. In *Newspaper Days*, a memoir written when he was 60, the man who became America's most feared and celebrated journalist describes his apprenticeship at the *Herald* as "the maddest, gladdest, damndest existence ever enjoyed by mortal youth." By then he was convinced that the newsroom, that battlefield where massed typewriters were the heavy ordnance, was the best and only education that could have made him what he was. "At a time when the respectable bourgeois youngsters of my generation were college freshmen, oppressed by simian sophomores and affronted by balderdash daily and hourly by chalky pedagogues, I was at large in a wicked seaport of half a million people. . . . I was laying in all the worldly wisdom of a police lieutenant, a bartender, a shyster lawyer, or a midwife."

He was especially proud of one of his German ancestors, Johann Burkhard Mencke, a rector of the University of Leipzig who lampooned his own profession in a pamphlet titled *The Charlatanry of the Learned*, published in 1715. Mencken was so fond of it that he commissioned an English translation and paid to have it published by Alfred Knopf. Over the years his disparagement of formal education and educators only became more ruthless and unrestrained. "Let us not burn the universities—yet," he wrote. "After all, the damage they do might be worse. . . . Suppose Oxford had snared and disemboweled Shakespeare! Suppose Harvard had set its stamp upon Mark Twain!" ("The average schoolmaster is and always must be essentially an ass," he also proclaimed, "for how can one imagine an intelligent man engaging in so puerile an avocation?")

In Mencken's case there's little indication that any form of envy was involved. That he could out-write and out-reason nearly all college graduates had long been proven to his satisfaction. He was not by nature much given to envy, or humility. Heaping scorn on the pedagogues seems to have been one of his principal pleasures, and his essays crackle with glee. "The Lower Depths," published in *The American Mercury* in 1925, was his disembowelment of a particularly simpleminded treatise on the purposes of teaching English, one compiled from a survey of 80 reputable scholars:

Overwhelming proof of a thesis that I have maintained for years, perhaps sometimes with undue heat: that pedagogy in the United States is fast descending to the estate of a childish necromancy, and that the worst idiots, even among pedagogues, are the teachers of English. It is positively dreadful to think that the young of the American species are exposed day in and day out to the contamination of such dark minds. What can be expected of education that is carried on in the very sewers of the intellect? How can morons teach anything that is worth knowing? . . . The sound thing, the sane thing and the humane thing to do with this pathetic herd of A.B.'s would be to take them out in the alley and knock them in the head.

Today we look back on several generations of iconoclasts who resorted to intemperate language of this nature, enriching the entertainment value, if not always the profundity, of our public discourse. Hunter Thompson and Curtis White are certainly among Mencken's descendants. But this street-tough invective, directed at some of the nation's most sacrosanct sacred cows, was a brand-new thing in Mencken's day—erudition and eloquence stripped of gentility and good manners. He invented this style, this tone, and dared his scandalized victims to respond in kind. Two years after he published "The Lower Depths," we find him unrepentant, still lobbing grenades and tear-gas canisters into the Groves of Academe. A highly publicized rash of undergraduate suicides in the spring of 1927 provoked one college president, John Martin Thomas of Rutgers, to suggest that one of the causes was "too much Mencken." Mencken replied that it was perfectly natural for "every intelligent student" to despair and to consider suicide, an impulse heightened by the "intellectual humiliations of a college education."

"What I'd like to see, if it could be arranged, would be a wave of suicides among college presidents," he wrote. "I'd be delighted to supply the pistols, knives, ropes, poisons and other necessary tools. Going further, I'd be delighted to load the pistol, hone the knives, and tie the hangman's knots. A college student, leaping uninvited into the arms of God, pleases only himself. But a college president, doing the same thing, would give keen and permanent joy to great multitudes of persons. I drop the idea, and pass on."

This Swiftian passage, Mencken at his most droll and fearless, was refreshing in 1927 and remains provocatively relevant today. The consensus is that he was at the height of his powers and influence in the late Twenties, the heyday of Babe Ruth and Al Jolson, before the stock-market crash and the Great Depression took so much of the starch out of the smug middle-class America he delighted in taunting and deflating. Reading Mencken at full throttle is an experience enhanced by an accurate mental picture of the man who was producing this unprecedented prose, an image of him at the actual moment of production. Fred Hobson reminds us that Mencken typed with the two-forefinger search-and-punch method, and clearly at a terrific speed, since he was known to deliver as many 5,000 words in a single day's work. Compared to typing with eight fingers and a command of the keyboard, search-and-punch demanded a spectacular expense of physical energy. It was a workout, a performance not unlike a boxer working out on the heavy bag. An athlete who could work 12 hours and produce 5,000 words, like the young Mencken, might have developed powerful biceps and forearms. The newsrooms of the Twenties were not air-conditioned. Picture Mencken red-faced, sweating profusely, a gleam in his eye, hammering an oily, ink-soaked machine that may have been literally too hot to touch, gleefully smashing icons and skewering every pompous professor, preacher, or politician who dared to cross his path.

The image is more than vaguely infernal. Dr. Thomas was not the only college president, in those days when most schools were church-affiliated, who saw the agnostic Mencken as the devil's advocate, if not his ambassador on earth. Mencken's brand of anticlerical, streetwise iconoclasm was the antithesis of everything these educators hoped to instill in the young Christian ladies and gentlemen under their charge. Naturally any association with Old Scratch was like catnip to Mencken. Though he wore tailored suits and stood on a great deal more personal dignity than he allowed his victims, he might have considered it a great lark to attend some formal function with a red forked tail attached between the black ones of his tailcoat.

The kind of newsroom education available to H. L. Mencken at the dawn of the Typewriter Century changed more than writing styles and class assumptions. Its graduates emerged with a radically different view of human nature and the human condition. According to Mencken and most modernist critics, nineteenth-century American literature was marked by excessive idealism and optimism—though you couldn't prove that by the century's greatest writers, say, Poe, Hawthorne, Melville, or Twain. But native idealism and optimism are virtues that rarely survive a working journalist's experience. At the age when undergraduates waltzed and played football, Mencken was at large in turn-of-the-century Baltimore, witnessing hangings and autopsies, factory fires and streetcar accidents, crushing poverty and violent crimes of every device. Most damaging of all, for the idealist (it wasn't Mencken who said that a cynic is an idealist with experience), is the way newspaper work exposes its initiates to the swordplay of self-interest, at its most naked and raw.

If the Christian scholar, in pursuit of middle-class morality, was taught to ask, "What would Jesus do?"—or at least Aristotle—a reporter was taught first to follow the money, wherever it might lead. He learned to determine who benefits, in most cases financially, from every public endeavor, new law or change in policy; he came to believe that most politicians, judges, and bureaucrats were owned outright or at least compromised by plutocrats and special interests. He learned to assume that everyone has an angle. And these harsh lessons would inform everything he wrote for the rest of his life, whether poetry or criticism, fiction or history. Newsroom reality subjected young men to a philosophical straitening, a teleological overhaul only slightly less thorough than the one experienced by soldiers in combat. Few Sunday-school illusions remained. The moral universes of the Puritan, the Victorian, even the transcendentalist, seemed pinched and pastel to a 19-year-old reporter who has seen a carriage horse and its driver atomized in a gas explosion, or the hellholes where cities warehoused the abandoned children of the very poor. The civic twaddle and patriotic buncombe of campaign and commencement speeches ring forever false once you've sniffed a few public orators at close range.

This was the education of Henry Mencken, who as a literary critic declared that Henry James "would have been vastly improved as a novelist by a few whiffs from the Chicago stockyards. . . . What he needed was intimate contact with the life of his own country."

Besides those whiffs of the stockyards that cured him of preciousness and Romantic notions—the making of a cynic, or at least a skeptic—the newsroom baccalaureate entered adulthood free of many of the stupidities (*bêtises* in Flaubert's lexicon) embedded in his national culture. It was a popular idea among turn-of-the-century intellectuals that all the worst prejudices and most poisonous received ideas of previous generations were transmitted, like viruses, by uninspired educators. Henry Adams, whose Puritan antecedents and Harvard pedigree epitomized everything Mencken distrusted, nevertheless strikes the same note in his celebrated memoirs: "The chief wonder of education is that it does not ruin everybody concerned in it, teachers and taught."

Bertrand Russell and George Bernard Shaw concurred, vehemently. Even so, Mencken was the extreme case, a gifted student who escaped the pedagogues at the age of 15 and never went back. If we consider that the high school where he excelled had recently been known as the Baltimore Manual Training School and was hardly sympathetic to literature or the liberal arts, and note also that he had published a well-reviewed book on Friedrich Nietzsche before he was 28, Mencken's view of himself as the purest, finest example of a self-manufactured intellectual does not seem vainglorious. He was the product of no institution, system, or tradition, which must account in part for his range and his unshakable independence. He was *sui generis*, even among writers bred in the newsroom.

What Mencken would have thought is a game too many have played, in the posthumous decades since he was last able to explain or defend himself. Like the Holy Bible, he was prodigious—one learned estimate is 5 million words—and vulnerable to many interpretations. But it's too easy to imagine what Mencken would think of the writing game today, as creative writing programs flourish and creative reading disappears—a discouraging landscape of many writers, few readers, and no

way for a serious writer to make a living unless, like any professor of academic arcana, he passes what he knows to the next
generation of initiates, who teach it in their turn. The same may
soon be true of journalism, which no one in Mencken's day had
ever thought of teaching as an academic subject.

"Read, write, think," the Sage of Baltimore, who acknowledged no sages, might have counseled young writers who
sought his advice. "Don't waste your time sitting at the feet
of some self-important has-been, or picking each other's
under-seasoned brains." Whether he would have been more
sympathetic to the simple question of survival, as it applies
to the wordsmiths of our century, is anyone's guess. Mencken
sometimes demonstrated compassion, but empathy was not
one of his strengths. Since the digital revolution and the typewriter's demise, with news jobs vanishing and print media
scrambling to save themselves with online strategies that have
yet to bear much fruit, it's grimly clear that few of the influential
writers of the mid-twenty-first-century, if any such exist, will
be graduates of the newsroom—of the H. L. Mencken School of
Life. There's little doubt it would have broken Mencken's heart
to see serious American writing once again in the clutches of
academia, from which he had given his all to free it forever.

What does he leave for us to consider, besides millions of
words marshaled in what many perceive as a martial manner,
but marshaled in a manner that resembles no other, before or
since? Winners of the *Baltimore Sun's* H. L. Mencken Writing
Award (for notably truculent columnists) used to be encouraged to visit Mencken's house at 1524 Hollins Street, sit in
his chair in the front room on the second floor, even touch
the keys of the sacred, ancient Corona that still rested on his
desk. Above and around them were shelf after shelf of books,
their spines carrying the names of the writers he encouraged

or eviscerated, friends and foes, the famous and the forgotten —F. Scott Fitzgerald, Sinclair Lewis, James Branch Cabell, Thomas Wolfe, Theodore Dreiser, Joseph Hergesheimer. Somewhere near the desk was a copy of his magnum opus *The American Language,* a dictionary of our native English, the remarkable result of his ambition to be remembered as not only the Jonathan Swift of the twentieth century but its Samuel Johnson as well. The office on Hollins Street served as a kind of shrine to the Typewriter Century, a modestly powerful memorial to the profession of letters in a bygone but eloquent era.

The City Life Museums of Baltimore closed the Mencken House in 1997. It sits empty now, threatened with demolition by soulless bureaucrats who can barely remember Johnny Unitas, far less the only sage with whom the city was ever credited. Mencken is still a source of civic pride for a few (older) Baltimoreans, who attend annual birthday speeches at his graveside and raise money to preserve his house. Their prospects for saving it are not considered encouraging. Does the indestructible Corona still sit there in the darkened room behind the locked doors, or has it been carried off by one of the faithful or, worst case of all, buried in a landfill?

Angry with His Own Time

T HE GREAT Austrian novelist Robert Musil, born like Mencken in 1880, placed these prophetic words in the mouth of his protagonist Ulrich, in *The Man without Qualities*: "One can't be angry with one's own time without damage to oneself." It's a warning H. L. Mencken may never have read, or have held up to him as a caution by a friend or an enemy, but it suits his case as well as anything he wrote or had written about him. He was a cultural and political malcontent who hurled anathemas left and right and aligned himself with no one. His favorite boast was that resistance to the status quo was in his bloodstream. "How did I get my slant on life?" he replied in an interview in 1926. "My ancestors for 300 years back were all bad citizens. . . . They were always against what the rest were for. . . . I was prejudiced when I came into the world."

It can be argued that this instinct for opposition was the making of Mencken, that it resonated with a restless minority of closet rebels who embraced him as their prophet and war-lord. It's certain, looking back on his career's trajectory, that he asserted it at a terrible cost to himself. Professionally he committed suicide twice, first when he sided with the kaiser in World War I, and second—beyond resurrection this time—when he failed to convince most Americans that he was suffi-ciently outraged by Hitler's Third Reich. He alienated another generation of potential readers with his pathological loathing of Franklin D. Roosevelt. Mencken never equivocated or apologized, of course. But he was conspicuously out of fashion by the age of 60, a fact that must have wounded him more than any of the verbal slings and arrows that failed to penetrate his armor-thick skin. His courage cannot be questioned. Every biographer, reviewing Mencken's attacks on God and country in times of feverish piety and patriotism, marvels that he was never lynched, or even physically assaulted.

At the beginning of the Great War in Europe, in 1914, he had remarked to Theodore Dreiser that he hoped to "spend my declining years in a civilized country." His distaste for the country of his birth seemed to peak in 1919—understandably, as the Red Scare metastasized, Prohibition loomed, and he remained muzzled and closeted by the *Baltimore Evening Sun*—when he wrote to his friend Gerald Boyd that he was "planning to get out of the United States as soon as possible, and to stay out." Earlier in the year he had advised Dreiser of his hope "to move to Munich as soon as I can shake off my obligations." But his dreams of romantic self-exile never materialized, to the delight of many and the chagrin of many more.

The wisdom of Musil's aphorism is not beyond question. Anger against their "own time" has always marked individuals of unusual insight or compassion. And which time in history, it's worth asking, has seen such a flowering of human excellence that most citizens would have declared themselves contented? Moreover, the "time" that belonged to Musil and Mencken was a time of unprecedented slaughter and devastation, of fascism, genocide, and two world wars that completed the collapse of European civilization. Happy warriors were few, and suspect. Joseph Roth, the brilliant Austrian novelist and journalist who combined the gifts of Musil and Mencken, had the terrible misfortune to be a Jew as well as a genius. Roth fled the Nazis and drank himself to death at the age of 45, in exile in Paris on the eve of the Second World War. (Musil, whose wife was Jewish, died an exile in Switzerland in 1942.) H. G. Wells, another disillusioned contemporary, died at the end of the war, a few months after publishing a last lament for Western civilization titled *Mind at the End of Its Tether.* Wells outdid them all by suggesting that the earth itself was fed up with the murderous human race and was in the process of rejecting it.

A dark view of the social order and the ideas that propped it up was hardly a strange reaction to the twentieth century. But what set Mencken apart from the Europeans was that his most outspoken revulsion against the established order came in times of peace and prosperity. The great wars crushed Europe, winners and losers alike, but they left the United States in an enviable position, for the first time in its brief history the most powerful and influential country in the world, and the most secure. Though Mencken was the grandson of German immigrants on both sides—his Mencken grandfather emigrated from Saxony in 1848—he was a full-fledged and somewhat pampered child of the American middle class. "Fat, saucy and contented" were the words he used to describe himself after a happy childhood as the eldest son of a prosperous tobacco merchant.

But if he was ever guilty of the bourgeois sin of contentment, it was not a sin he tolerated among his countrymen. If the prosperous Jazz Age America of Calvin Coolidge and bathtub gin was a sty of contentment, Henry Mencken was the stinging gadfly who kept the pigs awake.

"What one beholds, sweeping the eye over the land, is a culture that, like the national literature, is in three layers— the plutocracy on top, a vast mass of undifferentiated human blanks bossed by demagogues at the bottom, and a forlorn intelligentsia gasping out a precarious life between." Mencken wrote that in 1920, the year Warren G. Harding was elected to replace Woodrow Wilson in the White House. Nearly a century later, what would he behold, sweeping his gimlet eye over the land, that is so strikingly different? Only technology. The bloody twentieth was a century of revolutionary, life-altering technologies—automobiles, nuclear energy, and television in Mencken's time, computers in ours. Americans embraced each of these with reckless, simian enthusiasm, but each has proven to be a dangerously mixed blessing, with the worst perhaps yet to come. Through it all, Mencken's three-tiered culture has remained intact, cemented in place by technology that enabled the plutocrats to manipulate the helots more efficiently.

Mencken was a man of conservative temperament, born in the age of the horse and buggy, who lived into the age of hydrogen bombs and nuclear disarmament. It's no surprise that he was a devout technophobe who in his last, invalid years rejected television as hopelessly moronic. He had always detested the telephone, an archenemy of his privacy. "The greatest boon to bores ever invented," he called it. "The most infernal invention of the 20th century."

"The only modern inventions that have been of any real use to me are the typewriter and the Pullman car," Mencken announced to an interviewer in 1946. In spite of his professed allegiance to science, he was no gadgeteer. But it's precarious trying to isolate, precisely, just what it was about his time that most infuriated Mencken. This was not only the man who contradicted everyone, but a man who personally embodied a galaxy of contradictions, which is what has made him such a challenge for biographers and scholars. An educated guess is that the thing he loathed most was optimism. Animal optimism—animal spirits—he endorsed and enjoyed. Food and drink, sexual attraction, good music (as he defined it), good company, and good conversation were essential to his well-being. This was no sour ascetic or life-denying hermit. What he detested was delusional optimism, as he saw it— organized religion with its promises of ecstatic afterlife, the cult of human progress, American exceptionalism, popular beliefs in the essential goodness of humankind and the benevolence of representative democracy. It was this doctrine of the Ascent of Man, of cultural, moral, spiritual, and supernatural uplift, that never failed to raise his hackles and provoke his most venomous rhetoric.

Most educated people of Mencken's time, on both sides of the Atlantic, would have agreed that the ancient European culture was infinitely superior to the American brand, if in fact the USA could lay claim to any culture at all. Oscar Wilde's famous epigram, penned after a speaking tour of the United States in 1882, reinforced our inferiority complex: "America is the only country that went from barbarism to decadence without civilization in between." As a German American raised within an ethnic community, Mencken was a student, admirer, and staunch partisan of the Europeans, and of Germans in particular. The admiration was mutual. Biographer Marion Elizabeth Rogers credits European intellectuals and journalists as "the first to recognize his merits"—thanks in part, no doubt, to Mencken's poor opinion of American character and society, a prejudice most of them shared. *L'enfant terrible de la critique americaine* they called him in France. The deposed Kaiser Wilhelm, in exile in Holland, was an enthusiastic reader of Mencken's scathing *Notes on Democracy*, published in 1926, and sent him a framed photograph inscribed "With thanks for your splendid book on democracy."

The photograph was reportedly hung in the back hall on the third floor at 1524 Hollins Street. Even Mencken hesitated to scandalize his personal guests. But as he saw it, an unnecessary, fraudulently promoted war had ruined Germany and eclipsed a superior civilization—all to the great advantage of the United States, which, after virtually suspending the Bill of Rights to support its war effort, impudently embarked on a decade of optimism. The damn Yankees had the temerity to be pleased with themselves. For many middle-class Americans the Twenties were a time of giddy excess and self-congratulation, with nothing much but H. L. Mencken to spoil it for them. That theirs was a fool's paradise was proven, to Mencken's satisfaction, by the stock-market crash of 1929 and the brutal Depression that followed.

One of Europe's most enduring negative stereotypes, of the ugly or at least clueless American, was created in large part by Sinclair Lewis in his novels *Main Street* (1920) and *Babbitt* (1922), and by the novelist's most ardent supporter, the critic H. L. Mencken. Even today, many sophisticated Europeans see George Babbitt when they try to picture an American, and in most of what political scientists now call America's red states, they might not be far off the mark. Mencken referred to himself as "an old professor of Babbittry." In 1927 the English author/philosopher C. E. M. Joad, an influential voice of his day, published *The Babbitt Warren*, a savage critique of American society that rested entirely on Lewis's vision. It was no great surprise when the Swedish Academy made Lewis the first American winner of the Nobel Prize in Literature, in 1930. In the approving eyes of the Academy and most Continentals, Lewis and Mencken were bold cultural traitors whose great contribution was exposing the inferiority of their arrogant countrymen.

The fictional George Babbitt was more nuanced and prone to soul-searching than the stereotype he left behind, but it's the shallow, crassly materialistic conformist—the booster—that survived in the world's imagination. The linchpin of Babbitt's psyche, or of any booster's, was free-floating optimism—investment in The American Dream—and that was what rendered them so odious to Mencken. Though he raged against the booster's simple faith that any rich person was a person of consequence, money and property were by no means inconsequential to America's great skeptic. Ebenezer Scrooge's account book was no more scrupulous about credits and debits than Mencken's posthumously published autobiography (*My Life as Author and Editor*, 1993), where royalties from every edition of every book are recorded down to the last penny, literally: "my receipts from it amounted altogether to $3222.33." A dollar sign in some context appears on nearly every page. Though Mencken was never considered an astute businessman, in his various roles as editor, publisher, and best-selling author, he was never a careless or negligent one. At the cash register he was ever his father's son.

Several of Mencken's close friends, including Marcella du Pont of the royal family of Delaware and Fred and Betty Hanes of the North Carolina textile dynasty, were very wealthy indeed. He prized his invitations to visit their great estates, and he relished and meticulously reported his black-tie evenings at some of the stately homes of Old Virginia, among bluebloods like the writer James Branch Cabell and the Russian prince Pierre Troubetzkoy. His code of behavior for gentlemen, often reiterated in one form or another, did not neglect the homely bourgeois virtues of honoring every debt, paying bills on time, and living within one's means. As he well knew, these standards would have excluded a legion of writers and artists, from Villon to Joyce, and no few journalists (or aristocrats, for that matter). What Mencken detested in public was the American tendency—far worse among what passes for aristocracy in our time than it was in his—to pursue wealth as an end, not a means. He was of course very confident that he could tell the difference.

But American optimism had many faces besides the dime-store, Moose Lodge, rubes-at-the-county fair variety that stirred Lewis and Mencken to eloquent contempt. It's essential to remember that Henry Mencken grew up in the nineteenth century, a century when many Americans cast off the drab raiments of science and logic and embraced Mormonism, Rosicrucianism, theosophy, spiritualism, Christian Science, Millerism, and scores of exotic cults that provided a cynic with an infinitely target-rich environment. The gullible could choose from so many varieties of supernatural uplift, most of them replete with spirits and angels, that one foreign journalist described nineteenth-century American religion as "a mighty beating of wings." In this celestial landscape Mencken functioned like the Avenging Angel of Reason. Wherever words like "esoteric," "occult," or "hermetic" applied, you could find him with a blowtorch, scorching every winged thing that crossed his path. Mysticism in all its forms drove him to apoplexy. He dismissed it sourly as "an attempt to construct a non-Euclidean world in which anything that can be imagined is assumed to have happened."

Orthodox religions fared little better with the author of *Treatise on the Gods*. The adolescent Mencken and his brother Charlie had been sent to Methodist Sunday school to acquire the rudiments of Christianity, and as a result of this unwelcome exposure to mainstream Protestants he always singled out the poor Methodists for more than their fair share of ridicule. But no church, no sect, no religious tradition was spared. Like every Stoic and agnostic from Marcus Aurelius to Bertrand Russell and Friedrich Nietzsche, Mencken reconciled himself, early in life, to the fact that his own death would be followed by nothing but silence.

Imagine what a dreadful prospect eternal silence must have been, for H. L. Mencken. But if he was obliged to accept silence, what could be more galling than millions of cheerful Christians who expected to spend eternity singing in the heavenly choir, shouting hosannas and exchanging bon mots with Jesus and his saints? Eschatological optimism on this scale was unbearable to Mencken, who did everything he could to undermine the confidence of these giddy true believers. He was an admirer of the silver-tongued atheist Robert Ingersoll, and after Ingersoll no American could claim to have sowed and nurtured more religious doubt than the verbal arsonist from Baltimore. "Theology," he sneered, "is the effort to explain the unknowable in terms of the not worth knowing."

It's ironic that one of his best-known, most widely circulated quotes is his definition of Puritanism: "The haunting fear that someone, somewhere, may be happy." Apparently one of Mencken's haunting fears was that someone, somewhere, might have been happy because he was Saved. He was tireless in his disparagement of religion, leaving literally thousands of elegant little verbal grenades to be admired and launched at the faithful by future generations of agnostics. What they boil down to, stripped of wit and malice, is his firm belief that supernatural religion is thoroughly incompatible with an analytical, inductive sort of mind—a superior one, he would have said—and serves as a towering permanent barrier to the improvement of the species.

"Religion, like poetry, is simply a concerted effort to deny the most obvious realities," he insisted, and he admitted few distinctions between the more dignified, time-honored religions and the wild-eyed new theologies that bloomed and faded in the nineteenth century. He always blamed his split with Marion Bloom, the only woman he was known to love and court before his marriage at 50 to Sara Haardt, on Bloom's conversion to Christian Science. He took it as a personal insult when she tried to convert him to the Mary Baker Eddy heresy, a beguiling pseudoscience he scorned as "buncombe" and "pishposh." "Is she simply kidding me?" he agonized in a letter to Bloom's sister. "I surely hope so."

The word "faith" itself, describing optimism both boundless and groundless, was ever a burr under Mencken's saddle. "Faith may be defined briefly as an illogical belief in the occurrence of the improbable," he ruled. "A man full of faith is simply one who has lost (or never had) the capacity for clear and realistic thought. He is not a mere ass; he is actually ill. Worse, he is incurable."

Nor were the comforts of religion his only target, in his crusade to expose and destroy every stronghold of optimism in the United States, an exasperatingly buoyant nation if there ever was one. He reached adulthood at a time when two of America's most revered literary icons—the one populist, the other serving a more erudite and rarefied readership—were Walt Whitman and Ralph Waldo Emerson, prophets in their separate ways of soaring hope and optimism. Though he gave them both credit for helping to create a distinctly American voice for our literature, throwing off the shackles of the English tradition he professed to detest, they were predictably not to his taste. Whitman gets off with a light sentence, compared with many of the writers Mencken savaged; "trivial" was the worst adjective launched in his direction. But Mencken's contempt for Emerson and the transcendentalists—indeed, for any books or writers he associated with Harvard and New England—was a major theme in his literary criticism.

Even though transcendentalism had begun as a rebellion against calcified religion, and rejected the literal truth of Christianity, Mencken saw only more of the same in its high-flown idealism, affected language, and constant evocation of "spirit." In *Minority Report*, dispatching with the Eastern religion and philosophy that was enjoying a vogue at the time, he wrote, "I have found nothing in it save nonsense. It is, fundamentally, a moony transcendentalism as absurd as that of Emerson, Alcott and company." Emerson was precisely the kind of lofty Boston Brahmin that Mencken was always waiting to ambush, and several of his attacks seem singularly harsh. In the first book of *Prejudices*, he wrote, "The Emerson cult, in America, has been an affectation from the start," and ridiculed it as a passion of "chautauqua orators, vassarized old maids and other such bogus intelligentsia." But his animus is easier to understand when you consider that a core belief of the transcendentalists was the inherent goodness of people and nature, a belief that was like waving a red cape at a surly old bull like Mencken. And consider that Emerson once wrote, "Write it on your heart that every day is the best day of the year," a slice of refrigerator-magnet optimism that readers far less cynical than Mencken might find cloying.

In his speech "The American Scholar" (1837), Emerson invokes "the Divine Soul which inspires all men." We don't need to know more to understand that he and Mencken could never be reconciled. In the streets of Baltimore, the young Mencken was unable to channel any of the loftiness Emerson absorbed from the forests of New England. But the key to his quarrel with Emerson and Whitman is that they were not only optimists but devout humanists, the most influential humanist voices of their day. And then there was Mencken.

"What makes you believe that I am 'a friend of humanity'?" he once raged, responding to a reader who accused him of ignoring the crimes of the Third Reich. "As a matter of fact, I believe that humanity will deserve to be blown to hell." Perhaps the ultimate in antihumanist eloquence is achieved in this Mencken aphorism, published in the *Baltimore Evening Sun* in 1927: "Shave a gorilla and it would be almost impossible, at twenty paces, to distinguish him from a heavyweight champion of the world. Skin a chimpanzee and it would take an autopsy to prove he was not a theologian."

In the perpetual trial of the human race, for crimes against its own and every other life-form, H. L. Mencken was always a vigorous witness for the prosecution. There might be many reasons to take issue with Protagoras's pronouncement, "Man is the measure of all things," but to Mencken it was the measure of all things vain and foolish. Whenever philosophy or theology began to sound like what we today would call the self-help industry or the human potential movement, that's when he would turn his back and begin to count his bullets. "My first adventures as a reporter convinced me that the uplift in all its branches was only buncombe," the elderly Mencken recorded in his autobiography. It's frightening to think what he might have done with the twenty-first-century equivalent of Chautauqua, convention center–sized "Success" seminars that dispense the alleged wisdom of ex-presidents, evangelists, quarterbacks, basketball coaches, sales gurus, and exercise mavens in massive overdoses of the positive and the obvious that eager, unsuccessful simpletons pay hundreds of dollars to absorb.

Mencken's wars against the uplifters, the Norman Vincent

Peales, Billy Grahams, Oprah Winfreys, and Deepak Chopras of his day, still rouse cheers from the dour skeptics who read him faithfully. But in hindsight some of his literary and cultural antagonisms seem more personal and less persuasive. It's impossible to separate his rejection of Emerson ("the favorite metaphysician of Mary Baker Eddy") from his lifelong conviction that New England, from the *Mayflower* landing to Amy Lowell, was the source of a virus that enfeebled and feminized the national letters. Other literary critics condemned individual books and authors; it was Mencken's practice to condemn whole regions. In his gold-standard biography *Mencken: A Life* (1994), Fred Hobson speculates humorously about the Mencken Map of American Civilization, with vast regions blacked out as essentially subhuman. If we sum up the view from Baltimore, Hobson writes, "the only civilization in the United States seemed to rest in the Middle Atlantic states, from Maryland to New York, and perhaps that northern industrial belt between New York and Chicago—and, on the West Coast, San Francisco."

But unlike his high-spirited skewering of Midwestern Babbitts and Southern barbarians, Mencken's distaste for New England "Puritans" turned on class issues where his own superiority could not be taken for granted. Class consciousness is never irrelevant to a survey of Mencken's work. Both a snob and a sworn enemy of snobbery, he was perhaps too aware that he was not considered the social equal of Lowells and Cabots, and it planted a noticeable chip on his shoulder. Like the paranoid president Richard Nixon a generation later, Mencken saw Harvard and the Ivy Leaguers as an exclusive club where he could never be welcome, and was inclined to despise everyone on the other side of that closed door.

Clearly he protested too much. "There are more Ph.D.'s on

my family tree than even a Boston bluestocking can boast," he once boasted. "There was a whole century when even the most ignorant of my house was at least *Juris utriusque Doctor*." It's difficult for the reader, as it seemed difficult for the author, to separate his animosity toward Harvard, Puritans, Boston bluestockings, "the Genteel Tradition," and the Emersonians from his wholesale repudiation of universities, scholars, and his special target range of intellectuals headed by Harvard's Irving Babbitt, founding father of the New Humanism. Mencken sneered at this New Humanism, a great force among contemporary scholars, as "a religion without a God," and, worse, "the blood brother" of Rotarianism.

No humanist, old or new, escaped him unscathed. In his criticism Mencken stooped to ad hominem meanness—"the amusing but falsetto vituperations of Irving Babbitt" and the "Presbyterian metaphysics" of Princeton's Paul Elmer More. And in spite of his reputation for personal courtesy, especially toward women, Mencken could take these literary vendettas personally and behave churlishly in public. Stuart Sherman, a Harvard-bred scholar at the University of Illinois whose great sin in Mencken's eyes was denouncing Theodore Dreiser, approached Mencken at a dinner party and attempted to shake his hand, if not to bury the hatchet. Mencken refused his hand, and wrote to a friend that Sherman "seemed to me a swine."

His image as the cheerful, detached happy warrior of letters tends to fade under close inspection. And when he attacked literary critics like Babbitt and Sherman, he made enemies who were by no means verbally toothless. Though no one could match Mencken when it came to vitriol, sarcasm was not a world where he ruled alone. Babbitt scored a palpable hit when he described Mencken's free-swinging criticism as "intellectual vaudeville," and again when he reminded his adversary of a cautionary note from Gustave Flaubert: "By dint of railing at idiots, one runs the risk of becoming idiotic."

Even the rebuffed "swine," Sherman, deserves notice for some highly expressive (and not too hyperbolic) English prose in this response to one of Mencken's broadsides: "He leaps from the saddle with sabre flashing, stables his horse in the church, shoots the priest, hangs three professors, exiles the Academy, burns the library and the university, and amid smoking ashes, erects a new school of criticism on modern German principles."

Scholars like Babbitt and Sherman prayed to gods very different from the ones in Mencken's pantheon. But they were no fools or empty suits, and their replies to the abuse he heaped on them captured a real problem with Mencken's work. He hunted with an elephant gun, whether he was after big game—fear, war, ignorance, fossilized religion, hypocrisy, the shams of democracy—or merely fighting parochial battles against critics with different tastes. His choice of weapons and ammunition never varied, and when he hit a squirrel-sized target squarely, the scraps of meat that remained were barely enough to feed his readers. It's perhaps a point worth taking, in *A Book of Prefaces*, when Mencken charges that "the intolerable prudishness and dirty-mindedness of Puritanism" has, evolving over the centuries, "put an almost unbearable burden upon the exchange of ideas in the United States." But it didn't mobilize literary patriots to march on Harvard Yard or tear down the Pilgrim Monument at Plymouth, though Mencken's language will always sound as if that's what he had in mind.

At its most stentorian it verged on anti-intellectualism, and even if it was free of envy—he swore that envy was an emotion he had never experienced—his bitter engagements with the halls of ivy were far from the most convincing part of Mencken's program. If it's fair to say that he always confronted the ruling class, the dominant players in his world as he perceived them, it seems that he was prescient about politicians and plutocrats but inclined to overrate pedagogues. Then as now, serious ideas and the people who prize them play a small supporting role in the American melodrama. And when he blamed New England humanists and transcendentalists for the unhealthy growth of spiritual uplift and blind optimism in this country, Mencken risked exposing a blind spot of his own.

Most people who reject orthodox, dogmatic religion nevertheless recognize religious feelings in themselves and attempt—poetically, aesthetically, philosophically—to identify and express them. Psychological facts are relevant data, as William James argues in *Varieties of Religious Experience*, and need to be taken into account. It isn't all nonsense because you can't see it, touch it, weigh it, quantify it. People are naturally drawn to the mystical and supernatural—the "woo-woo," in modern slang—but they're responding to something besides the need to fool themselves. Self-deception often follows close behind, but extra-rational perceptions—intimations of immortality, in Wordsworth's language—are something more than a fatuous waste of time and mind.

So many of us would argue. But Mencken, like Richard Dawkins and some of our contemporary atheists, thoroughly disagreed. Mencken disagreed, apparently, because he had no such feelings. To be grounded in science and wed to common sense, as he was and we all should be, still leaves some narrow options. Scornful rejection of everything extrasensory may not be the most enlightened of those options. A peril of the scientific intellect is literal-mindedness, and if Mencken suffered any intellectual disability it was that one. There were notes on the scale of human experience that his ear did not pick up. When biographers tell us that he saw little to admire in James Joyce,

Herman Melville, or T. S. Eliot, we're forced to conclude that his critical range was not unlimited.

Mencken was right to defend Dreiser, whose naturalism was subjected to priggish and condescending criticism from academic critics. "The Genteel Tradition" was a concept introduced by philosopher George Santayana, in an effort to distance himself from what he viewed as a wan academic idealism at Harvard, a timid conformity that stifled the growth of philosophy and literature. (Santayana, unlike Mencken, was a harsh critic of America who walked the walk; shortly after delivering his famous lecture on the Genteel Tradition [1911], he resigned from Harvard's faculty, left the country, and never returned.) If one free interpretation of that tradition was that it ignored or marginalized the lives of the poor and undereducated—the vast majority of Americans—Mencken and his allies were on firm ground when they joined in denouncing it. But the distinguished Southern critic Louis Rubin Jr. makes a convincing case that Mencken had more or less abandoned literature before he turned 50. For all the incalculable influence he had exerted on a generation of readers who grew up before the Depression, it's likely that his passion lay elsewhere. The great auto-didact, the boy from vocational school, had succeeded in shaking the very foundations of the House of Letters, declared himself satisfied, and moved on.

His most enduring contribution may prove to be his comprehensive analysis, cruel but penetrating, of the prevailing Mind of America. This is also true of Santayana, another skeptic of the national optimism, who described Ralph Waldo Emerson as "a cheery, child-like soul, impervious to the evidence of evil." But Santayana abandoned us while Mencken, always insisting that the democratic spectacle was his favorite entertainment, stuck with us to the end. Wherever the tree of hopefulness grew too vigorously, he was there with his pruning shears to trim it back. He was described as the nation's astringent, and also as its emetic.

Against the proofs that he was always "angry with his time," there is the argument that a man like Henry Mencken would have been angry with any time, or any place. But if he were here today to instruct us, as was his habit, he would point to the dreadful symmetry of our follies as he chronicled and predicted them. We were on the winning side in two wars, and each of them was followed by Red Scares and communist witch hunts, the notorious Palmer Raids in 1919–1921, and the equally notorious reign of Senator Joe McCarthy after World War II. These paranoid periods were characterized by jingoism, censorship, grotesque hypocrisy, and the righteous suspension of most of the liberties of which America loves to boast. Mencken would have nodded his head, ruefully, at the Patriot Act and the war on terrorism with its constitution-defying domestic spying, all spawned by the bombings of September 2001. Coddle them and they love freedom, he would have said; kick them and they destroy it.

The postwar paroxysms of unreason and injustice were both followed by periods of boundless optimism—the Twenties and the Fifties—as if the American populace, after the arrests and deportations and ruined lives, was somehow pleased with itself instead of ashamed. Mencken must have judged it a misfortune that he lived on into the happy-face Fifties, the age of Ike and Mamie and Ozzie and Harriet. Followed, of course, by a decade of assassinations and a humiliating war that America did not win. But Mencken was never shy about saying "I told you so."

The Word at War

T HE MOST significant, most personal and moving endorsement of H. L. Mencken by any major writer may be this paragraph from *Black Boy*, by Richard Wright:

> A block away from the library I opened one of Mencken's books and read a title: *A Book of Prefaces*. I was nearing my nineteenth birthday and I did not know how to pronounce the word "preface." I thumbed the pages and saw strange words and strange names. I shook my head, disappointed. I looked at the other book; it was called *Prejudices*. I knew what that word meant; I had heard it all my life. And right off I was on guard. . . . That night in my rented room, while letting the hot water run over my can of pork and beans in the sink, I opened *A Book of Prefaces* and began to read. I was jarred and shocked by the style, the clear, clean, sweeping sentences. Why did he write like that? And how did one write like that? . . . He was using words as a weapon, using them as one would use a club. Could words be weapons? Well, yes, for here they were. Then, maybe, perhaps, I could use them as a weapon? No. It frightened me. I read on and what amazed me was not what he said, but how on earth anybody had the courage to say it.

Apparently Mencken appreciated it, because a copy of *Black Boy*, with this passage marked out, was found in his library after his death. Words as weapons. Hardly a new concept—Emile Zola wrote *J'accuse*, indicting the whole French nation, when Mencken was 18 years old. Strong language that challenged authority was nothing new in 1517, when Martin Luther nailed his *Ninety-Five Theses* to the church door in Wittenberg. But it startled America when the boy editor from Baltimore began to open fire in all directions, ending what seemed like a gentleman's agreement among America's Victorians to be civil and respectful of the powers that be.

It's no surprise that it was especially startling to Wright, a black man raised in a society where a defiant word or gesture could provoke white people to kill him. Though he no doubt inspired and gave courage to America's oppressed and downtrodden, Mencken himself was notably unsympathetic to their plight. "The world gets nothing from him save his brute labor, and even that he tries to evade," from *Notes on Democracy*, is a mild example of his affection and respect for the proletarian. Nor, unlike his friend Theodore Dreiser, the twelfth of 13 children born to an immigrant's wife, was he in any sense downtrodden himself. As the favored eldest son of a successful businessman, he was raised in a permissive, encouraging middle-class home where he never missed a meal. His comfortable origins always set biographers off in search of the mystery of his belligerence. Never cornered or abused in his life, humiliated but once on record—by a four-term president of the United States—he nevertheless fought his battles like a cornered, wounded wolverine.

What drove this cigar maker's son to deploy the English language as his private arsenal, an armory richly stocked with explosive devices, with objects blunt and sharp to bruise, to pierce the skin of the wretches who offended him? His love of exotic and archaic words reminds us of some sophisticated assassin, bored with the dagger and the garrote, picking up a crossbow or a scimitar and hefting it lovingly. Mencken once boasted that "The Free Lance," his first daily column for the *Baltimore Sun*, "launched me as a general assassin."

We can't accept uncritically his standard denial of any personal or emotional involvement in his polemics, a claim restated in his autobiography as he looked back on 40 years of combat: "My own stock of malice is rather under than above the average, for I am almost devoid of any capacity for either envy or moral indignation." Declaring rhetorical warfare on every icon and hallowed delusion of the society you live in, and attacking them daily for decades, is not some sport you take up for cardiovascular health, like tennis or cycling. There was a rage in Mencken, or at the least some simmering resentment. But it's a mistake to doubt that he enjoyed himself, to underestimate the sheer pleasure of offending the simpleminded and the doctrinaire (often the same), of "stirring up the animals" as he liked to say. As every columnist learns, it's much easier to offend everyone than to please everyone, and conducive to better writing, as well. The very worst of opinion-mongers are the ones who sit the fence and court general approval, followed in order of impotence by the pathetic eunuchs who write to please a partisan minority.

Those of us who have patiently sharpened a verb or an adjective, and heard its odious victim squeal aloud, have tasted some of the sweet fruit of life. Of course it helps to grow thick skin, in case the victim survives and fires back. Not all of us are sheathed in rhino hide like H. L. Mencken. Among writers with a license and an inclination to kill, malicious critics of literature, theater, and the fine arts have been common ever since Mencken showed them the way. A single choice, poisoned word in a prestigious publication can destroy the dreams of a playwright, the livelihood of a dozen actors, and the small fortune of a play's hopeful angel, and critics who never hesitated to exercise that power have flourished. Except for born SOBs, this guillotining of artists and would-be artists is a young person's game, and some of us who played it will go to our graves burdened with (mild) guilt from our youthful malevolence.

As a critic Mencken preferred a much grander stage, no less than man's estate and the metastatic folly of the human race. On this stage polemicists confront injustice, inequality, corruption, stupidity, cruelty. They're driven by indignation, which Mencken trivialized as moralizing, yet it fuels most political commentary. So what fueled the gorgeous invective of the silver-tongued bully from Baltimore? We can fairly judge that it was contempt, in large measure. But is contempt, a relatively arid emotion, a well deep enough to produce these millions, these tidal rivers of harsh words? Isolating Mencken's resentments is an exercise in smoke detection. Wherever the fires of his contempt appear to burn too intensely, where he seems to waste live ammunition on victims already supine, that's where we look to question his dispassion.

Take institutions of higher learning, to begin with. No doubt they were deficient and arrogant in his day, much as in ours. Yet his proposals to euthanize PhDs and bury them in common graves goes uncomfortably beyond tongue-in-cheek, at least on its tenth repetition, and we're reminded that Mencken never matriculated. We doubt that he often suffered condescension on this account, as he was a combative man who went about fully armed—verbally—and a man who had achieved considerable sway in his own world at an age when undergraduates were still writing term papers. But he was a proud man, and just the idea that they were thinking of condescending to him would have been sufficient to set him off. His relationship with the Harvard-bred Charles Angoff, his assistant at *The American Mercury*, was a curious one that seems to have involved constant baiting of the young man by the older one, with the theme that Angoff was prissy and unworldly, and easily shocked. According to Angoff's memoir, this baiting included Mencken urinating loudly and visibly with the door to the men's room open. Readers of Angoff's book may decide that he was not altogether undeserving of this abuse, or this reputation. The equation is complicated, however, by the fact that he was a Jew forced to listen to Mencken stereotyping Jews.

Angoff, with his cloistered education and religious awe of the writer's art, was the perfect anti-Mencken, the perfect foil, God's gift to Angoff's sardonic master. But what Mencken professes is often called into question by what Mencken reveals, somewhere on the groaning bookshelf that is his legacy. His disdain for literary aestheticism seems undermined to a degree by his lifelong intoxication with language itself. Mencken's archives include composition books from his earliest schooling, and Fred Hobson notes that one of his projects as a grammar school student at Knapp's Institute was to translate the word "man" into 26 languages, several of them imaginary. It's also notable that German was his poorest subject at Knapp's, where most of the students were German Americans. English was his native language, the one spoken in his father's home. It was with industry and passion, not college course work or an ethnic advantage, that he mastered his ancestral language well enough—by his mid-twenties—to read Friedrich Nietzsche in the original German and publish a book on his philosophy (1907).

An apparent anomaly in Mencken's vast oeuvre is his remarkable dictionary, *The American Language*, a triumph of linguistic scholarship first published in 1919 and reprinted several times since, in expanded, abridged, and revised versions. If the prevailing flavor of his life and work was contentiousness—a preparation for combat, a state of siege—this masterwork of lexicography is disarmingly professorial and nonconfrontational. Perhaps its relative neutrality is misleading. Just as a white hunter, anticipating the charging rhinoceros, might obsess over the quality of his firearms, a born polemicist like Mencken needed assurance that he would never arrive at the verbal battlefront outgunned. The range and ambition of his dictionary are intimidating. We could read *The American Language* as Mencken's hubristic declaration that he *owned* American English, and that anyone who dared to use it against him was poaching at great peril.

By his own account, most things about America amused or disgusted Henry Mencken. Its language was a cardinal exception. It fascinated him to observe and chronicle a vigorous New World vernacular as it evolved. No doubt Mencken saw his war with America's scholars as a kind of Promethean triumph—he, the self-educated outsider, had stolen their most potent weapons, their fine polished words, and used those words against them. A man of no mean self-regard, he would have relished the Promethean metaphor, the theft of fire from the intellectual Olympus of Harvard and Yale. The dons, overmatched at their own game, outpreached in their own church, would gladly have chained him to a rock and called in the vultures.

It's a gross insult to Mencken's memory that an organization called the H. L. Mencken Club is now listed as a white supremacist "hate group" by the Southern Poverty Law Center. The "Club" is a gang of aging right-wing academics who couldn't burn a hot cross bun without setting their robes on fire. But there's no question that a much whiter, if not all-white, America is their common dream. A spokesman for the SPLC calls the Club "a kinder, gentler Klan." The insult—and the irony—is double. Not only was Mencken an early, outspoken, and formidable enemy of lynch law and night riders, but it's still a toss-up whether he despised the KKK any more than he despised the MLA. Klan robes and academic gowns were much the same to Henry Mencken.

He was no racist—he scorned all races equally, with special animus for those who believed themselves superior. But it must be conceded that he was guilty of what we can delicately call heightened ethnic consciousness (worth addressing at greater length further on). Even though German Americans like Mencken ranked above most other Europeans on nineteenth-century America's scale of social status, it was clear that they ranked below the Anglo-Saxons, and further below if they were but a generation or two from Ellis Island. It did not suit Mencken, who claimed noble blood and academic distinction among his German ancestors, to be ranked below anyone at all. His distaste for Anglo-Americans and their British cousins reached such a pitch that he openly supported Germany in World War I, which would have destroyed any career less illustrious than his own, and then hesitated to denounce Hitler for so long that he finally alienated his readership and removed himself from the national conversation.

Were these particular prejudices, insofar as they undercut Mencken's self-image as a calm and rational observer, nurtured by personal resentments he would have dismissed as unthinkable? If anyone had suggested to Mencken that envy, even in some subconscious Freudian form, had ever triggered his broadsides, the Sage would have kicked him down the stairs. But his most obvious and persistent resentment is one most thoughtful readers find sympathetic, and in many cases share and endorse. Mencken blustered and exaggerated and was not always candid, but there's one issue where you can take his every word at face value, and that issue is freedom. Though his conservatism would fail most of the tests imposed by the modern Right, he embodied to the highest degree what Ford Madox Ford, in his *Parade's End* tetralogy, memorably described as "the passionate Tory sense of freedom."

Everyone who has it, who feels it, knows immediately what Ford is expressing. The emotion is "Tory" in Ford's purview because as recently as the nineteenth century only the landed gentry had ever enjoyed enough freedom to develop a libertarian philosophy. But what it captures is the horror experienced by any person of independent mind and spirit when he finds his life controlled, or even substantially altered, by the whims of his inferiors—kings, dictators, or, perhaps worst of all for the Tory, the random, roiling mob. It provokes existential claustrophobia, an almost physical sense of being suffocated by stupidity. If you've never read a thorough study of this sensation and the conditions that cause it, you've never read H. L. Mencken on the subject of democracy.

There are times, reading Mencken, when we feel that too much time has passed, when this author whose work was primarily topical seems to recede into history. He was already a working journalist when Queen Victoria died; he was a contemporary of Theodore Roosevelt, Thomas Edison, John D. Rockefeller, Thomas Hardy. It has been many decades since another writer used the word "wowser," perhaps Mencken's favorite pejorative noun. Thanks to him it was a household word in his day, a satisfying slangy sobriquet for the worst kind of censorious Puritan, but now it requires a footnote. (It originated in Australian English, and the Australian writer

C. J. Dennis defined "wowser" as "an ineffably pious person who mistakes this world for a penitentiary and himself for a warder.") But when we reopen *Notes on Democracy*, the book that warmed the homesick heart of the exiled Kaiser Wilhelm in 1926, is seems as if no time has passed at all, and our Mencken might be fulminating on the op-ed page of tomorrow's *New York Times*.

Repetition, exaggeration and all, *Notes* rings as true in 2014 as it did in 1926. The plutocracy still rules the American roost, herding the masses far below them—"undifferentiated human blanks" in Menckenese—through the practiced demagoguery of hired herdsmen masquerading as public servants. "The American people, true enough, are sheep," he rages. "Worse, they are donkeys. Yet worse, to borrow from their own dialect, they are goats. They are thus constantly bamboozled and exploited by small minorities of their own number, by determined and ambitious individuals, and even by exterior groups. The business of victimizing them is a lucrative profession, an exact science, and a delicate and lofty art." And Mencken never lived to meet the Koch brothers, to seethe at the Supreme Court's decision in the Citizens United case, to see consultants, pollsters, and spin doctors turn every political candidate into a marionette, to witness the reconquest of the South by new demagogues pandering to old racists.

Mencken painted with broad strokes. In his tirades against mob rule, he made it clear that he thought decency was inseparable from intelligence. He would have challenged you if you objected that while all fundamentalists must be gullible, they aren't all witch-burners and bigots. But his take on "the people" is uncomfortably convincing. "Public opinion, in its raw state, gushes out in the immemorial form of the mob's fears," he sneers in *Notes on Democracy*. "It is piped to central factories, and there it is flavored and colored, and put into cans." This is unanswerable, vintage Mencken, cutting words with serrated edges. His incineration of the lamest of all democratic clichés, "the wisdom of the people," is no less compelling. "The democratic politician, confronted by the dishonesty and stupidity of his master, the mob, tries to convince himself and all the rest of us that it is really full of rectitude and wisdom," he writes. "The notion that the mob is wise, I fear, is not to be taken seriously: it was invented by mob-masters to save their faces."

Nearly a century after Mencken warned us, journalists take it for granted that anyone who says "the people know best" is trying to get away with something. Mencken's curse on democracy is not provisional. "The rule of the majority," he concludes thunderously, "must tend toward a witless and malignant tyranny, anti-social in its motives and evil almost beyond endurance in its effects." Those are weapon-words wielded by a warrior in high dudgeon and martial posture. A patriot might protest that other states—Italy, Mexico, and India, for example—have devised democracies even more dysfunctional than America's. But you don't have to share Mencken's apocalyptic pessimism to grasp that this is not a gleeful satirist expending his precious ammunition on easy targets. This is an anxious libertarian gasping for air—a libertarian who has seen, during the Wilson administration, what happens to civil liberties when a patriotic mob and its masters get a war between their teeth. His other books of this period, like *Treatise on the Gods* and *In Defense of Women*, are in the familiar Mencken spirit. The author is enjoying himself, inviting your envy of his superior logic and his superior English prose. *Notes on Democracy* is different. The man who betrayed no fear of Franklin Delano Roosevelt, Woodrow Wilson, the Ku Klux Klan, or the Judeo-Christian God of Our Fathers is conceding his fear of the mob—the *canaille*.

His rendering of the mob-man isn't designed to provoke a smirk, but a chill: "Behind all the great tyrants and butchers of history he has marched with loud hosannas, but his hand is eternally against those who seek to liberate the spirit of the race. . . . In two thousand years he has moved an inch: from the sports of the arena to the lynching party."

Not that he intended to give the bastards an inch. This may be the best of Mencken, man of many paradoxes, of many faces—the impassioned Tory waving his flag of freedom at the threatening, gaping mob. It's as close as he ever came to deliberate involvement in the political system. Even if democracy was a lost cause, this writer sincerely hoped his readers would agree with him, and reorder their thinking accordingly. Mencken's personal freedoms might be at stake. Of course there's substantial irony in the image of H. L. Mencken as a standard-bearer for anything, even liberty. We think of the French Revolution, with its motto "Liberté, Egalité, Fraternité," and we realize Mencken would have endorsed just the first of the three. Maybe he never actually said, "Bugger Egalité and Fraternité!," but he could have. To a man of his temperament, any revolution reeked to high heaven of the mob. "I have witnessed, in my day, the discovery, enthronement and subsequent collapse of a vast army of uplifters and world-savers," he wrote in the introduction to *Notes*, "and am firmly convinced that all of them were mountebanks."

All this is invigorating if you're a cynic who agrees with him, aggravating and depressing if you're an idealist who doesn't. We can appreciate Mencken's prose and his panache, take pleasure in his keenest insights, applaud when his mortar shells detonate a worthy target—all without pardoning his chronic overkill and his mistakes, his narrow tolerance. He still attracts admirers and deserves them, but it's best to beware of someone who calls himself a Menckenite. Those sad fools in the Mencken Club, who ended up on a list of hate groups? That's what comes of reading Mencken selectively, cherry-picking for your personal prejudices, and reaching predetermined conclusions. No doubt all the Clubmen are at least nominal Republicans and firm believers in laissez-faire capitalism who have overlooked, or forgotten, two of Mencken's more provocative proclamations. First, "In this world of sin and sorrow there is always something to be thankful for; as for me, I rejoice that I am not a Republican." And second, "Perhaps the most revolting character that the United States ever produced was the Christian businessman."

So much for our cult of right-wing neo-Menckenites, who would have found the flesh-and-blood H. L. Mencken no more congenial than our Christian businessmen would have found Jesus Christ, the illiterate Hebrew rabble-rouser. It's been the fate of many political thinkers—John Locke and Edmund Burke come to mind—to be immortalized chiefly by conservatives who willfully misunderstand them. How would Mencken view his own legacy, the long-term influence of a man who used words as weapons more skillfully, and for a larger audience, than any American writer before or since? He might agree that his greatest contribution was to the understanding, if clearly not the reform, of America's profoundly flawed political system. His distaste for populism and his grave concern for his personal liberties and those of his (few) peers are entirely in line with the philosophy of the Founding Fathers, as anyone who cares to do the reading can confirm.

When his quiver is empty, when every arrow has been launched and ideally found its mark, even the mightiest warrior of words faces the truth that he has shed no blood and sacked no cities, that his battles have been peripheral to the endless bloody, dirty, graceless wars fought by sociopaths and fools. Henry Mencken was not a man of action but a man of words, and like most of his tribe he probably died doubting that the pen is mightier than the sword. What of his chosen targets? The Ivy League and the Anglo-Saxon seem as entrenched today as they were in his heyday. Wars of intervention bleed us white. Fundamentalists multiply and still disparage Darwin, and a Mormon has run for president of the United States. Democracy and the wisdom of the people are still the sacred cows, long since swaybacked, barren, and dry-uddered, to which nearly every American, left or right, mindlessly genuflects.

If the pen was ever mightier than the sword, in America it was much weaker than the dollar. Words are magical, potent, and transformative only for those, like Richard Wright, who love and respect them—an endangered minority in this venal, gadget-infested consumer society where wealth trumps wit and wisdom at every turn. The spectacle of H. L. Mencken versus America is, finally, a humbling memory for pundits and social critics, for journalists who have fought with live ammunition against the status quo. No one ever came to that battlefield better equipped, more heavily armed with eloquence and attitude, than the troublesome man they called the Sage of Baltimore. He opened fire well over a century ago. Yet nearly everything about America that he loathed and ridiculed survives him.

"I Remain a Foreigner"

IN THIS twenty-first century, the liberal-minded define themselves as fully evolved citizens of the world, long since blind to such ephemeral distinctions as race, ethnicity, gender, or "sexual orientation." It's a test of membership in this civilized elite to betray no hint of prejudice or stereotyping on any occasion, not even when some representative of an oppressed minority sins grievously against decency or common sense. The more militant and self-righteous function as the language police, the "politically correct" vigilantes who pounce on every public violation of the unwritten code. The careers of politicians, entertainers, and athletes, who rarely belong to the broad-minded elite, can be destroyed or compromised overnight by one prejudiced outburst, one word or sentence that appears to betray the bigot within. Since America still harbors a great sufficiency of bigots and careless simpletons, a fresh example of this censorship makes news every day. The Internet serves as a devastating modern version of the Puritans' stocks, where the offending bigot is exhibited in his shame from coast to coast.

None of this was true in H. L. Mencken's day, not during any part of a career that spanned five decades. If there was a single distinction on which he prided himself, it was that he, like so few he acknowledged around him, was thoroughly "civilized."

It's the word he uses repeatedly to separate America's sheep from her goats. In most of Mencken's rants against demagogues, boosters, "wowsers," Prohibitionists, Bible-thumpers, and, indeed, bigots, we can clearly see where he draws the line, where civilization begins and where it ends, and we readily accept him as our surveyor. And then we pick up one of his books, or a book written about him, and find a Mencken quote like this one, from *Treatise on the Gods*: "The Jews could be put down very plausibly as the most unpleasant race ever heard of. As commonly encountered, they lack many of the qualities that mark the civilized man: courage, dignity, incorruptibility, ease, confidence. They have vanity without pride, voluptuousness without taste, and learning without wisdom. Their fortitude, such as it is, is wasted upon puerile objects, and their charity is mainly a form of display."

We wince, of course. We cringe. One thing Mencken, prescient in many ways, would not have predicted was that 60 years after his death no remotely "civilized" person anywhere could endorse such a primitive display of prejudice. Nor was this the larval Mencken writing, a callow youth who had not yet shaken off the nineteenth century. *Treatise* was published when he was 50 years old, at the height of his fame and his powers. Stranger yet, it was published by his close friend Alfred Knopf, a Jew. (Knopf requested the deletion of this passage from the manuscript before he reissued the book in 1946, and Mencken complied.) In those salad days of the Twenties his partner at the *American Mercury* was George Jean Nathan, a Jew, and his editorial assistant was Charles Angoff, Jewish also. It seems he was sitting at his desk surrounded by Jews, typing up anti-Semitic literature. This not only suggests egregious insensitivity on the part of Henry Mencken, but something much more disturbing—that in 1930 no American Jew was in a position to object to such an outrageous insult, not when it was the opinion of such a famous gentile.

Mencken's Jewish problem has been the focus of a posthumous movement to all but expunge him from the national literature. That movement gained momentum with the publication of his diaries in 1989, and many more adherents in 1991 when the Pratt Library in Baltimore, according to his instructions, opened the boxes he had sealed in 1956 and released the memoir titled *My Life as Author and Editor*. Edited by Jonathan Yardley, the book is less than revelatory, but it presents us with a Bartleby-like Mencken alter ego who recorded every dollar he ever earned or spent—and plenty of new material to indict him as an anti-Semite. It was no surprise, but it was ample corroboration of all the charges brought against him as America began to raise its multicultural consciousness.

Some readers of *My Life* were more shocked by his casual recall of a dinner with the bohemian Carl Van Vechten, one of the admirable racial liberals of the Twenties, whose circle of friends in New York included black writers and musicians. "I had to make him promise solemnly that there would be no blackamoors at table," Mencken wrote, "for though Sara had shaken off most of her native Alabama *Kultur*, she still declared that dining with them would make her uneasy." Mencken's tenderness toward his invalid wife has always registered as one of his most attractive traits, but this reality of Mr. and Mrs. Mencken as a couple indisposed to interracial dining dispels a great deal of their charm. He refers to poor Van Vechten's African American friends as "the more raffish intellectuals of the race," and describes his wife as a "peppery Russian Jewess." Van Vechten's hints that he might have been bisexual were so distasteful to Mencken that he dismissed them out of hand. Mencken, of course, was a devout homophobe who referred to Oscar Wilde's louche lover, Lord Alfred Douglas, as "a filthy homo."

There is no comfortable, defensible way to defend Mencken. Before you can try to explain or rehabilitate him, you have to go all the way down with him, and that can be way, way down. Was there any race, religion, or ethnic group that he did not, at some point, disparage? He was in fact a full-service misanthrope whose most defining quote may be this one: "The human race is incurably idiotic." The smothering blanket of his contempt for the entire species may render him less demonic than writers whose bigotry was more focused. Nathaniel Hawthorne was an antebellum Copperhead who deplored abolitionists and thought African slaves were fortunate to have owners to care for them. One of America's most revered memoirists was Henry Adams, author of *The Education of Henry Adams*, around which many a college course in American literature has been admiringly constructed. Adams also wrote, "The whole rotten carcass is rotten with Jew worms," which might have made H. L. Mencken catch his breath.

What did Jews ever do to offend Henry Adams, Boston Brahmin, son and grandson of American presidents? But George Bernard Shaw, H. G. Wells, T. S. Eliot, and Mencken's friend Theodore Dreiser would all be included on the long roster of serious writers and intellectuals who denigrated Jews. The late David Markson, the underappreciated author of experimental novels like *Wittgenstein's Mistress*, seasons his novel *Reader's Block* with terrible things famous people said about the Chosen People, so many and so nasty that an innocent reader has to pause and clear his head of the gathering poison. Way out in the Right field of gifted but logically damaged literary artists, we encounter anti-Semitic fanatics like Ezra Pound and Louis-Ferdinand Céline.

We expect those writers we admire to rise above the ignorance and prejudice of their time, but on close inspection most of them disappoint us. All evidence to the contrary, Mencken never saw himself as an anti-Semite. "I had little if any prejudice against Jews myself," he writes in *My Life*, "and in fact spent a great deal of my leisure in their company." Most of his Jewish friends and colleagues—with the notable exception of the Judas Angoff—supported this surprising self-assessment. To the end of his life, Alfred Knopf denied vehemently that Mencken was prejudiced; the daughter of Philip Goodman, the 300-pound beer-hall crony who played a kind of Jewish Falstaff to Mencken's Prince Hal, remembered her father's celebrated friend as "one of the most free and unbigoted of men." In Sara Mayfield's charming but conspicuously hagiographic memoir, she indignantly rejects "the preposterous charges than Mencken was a racist, pro-Nazi, and anti-Semitic."

He inspired loyalty, at any rate. Sara Mayfield clearly saw him as a lovable, avuncular figure, the kind of courtly older gentleman women refer to as a "pussycat." From the composite portrait of H. L. Mencken, this haze of paradox never lifts. But in Mencken's case we can't detach the nature of the man from a critical appreciation of his work. We can't grant him a literary free pass like Hawthorne or Eliot, whose work has virtually nothing to do with their social or political eccentricities, ugly as some of them may have been. After an early, undistinguished stab at poetry, Mencken was primarily a reactive (rather than reactionary) writer, a professional adversary whose subject matter was determined by the breaking news stories and public controversies of his day. He was a literary attack dog, the only one of real interest America ever produced, and it's intensely relevant to understand just whom he had trained himself to bite, and why. A polemicist whose best prose is derogatory and belligerent rests his reputation on posterity's judgments of his friends and foes.

It's accurate but insufficient to say that bigotry was gauged differently in those days. The Irish historian R. F. Foster, who wrote a critically acclaimed biography of William Butler Yeats, sagely advises biographers to begin with a close study of the world, and the specific cultural milieu, at the time their subject was 20 years old. H. L. Mencken was 20 in 1900, and the world he found around him was a world of immigrants. Changes occur so rapidly in the age of technology that Americans forget their country is only 225 years old—three average human lives stretched end to end cover our entire history. The middle man could have been cradled by a predecessor born in 1789, and himself cradled a successor still alive in 2014. In 1900, roughly halfway through its brief life span, the United States was on the crest of a colossal, unprecedented wave of European immigration. At that time 20 percent of the US population was foreign-born, compared to just 10 percent today. In the next decade, 1900–1910, immigration increased the population by 1 percent every year, a total of nearly 9 million new Americans who settled for the most part in the larger cities of the Eastern Seaboard.

That was Mencken's world at 20—the American melting pot was filling up rapidly, but the melting had not yet begun. Few of the new immigrants spoke English. Each urban neighborhood was like a tiny foreign country, with its own language, dress, food, and folklore. Each enclave was foreign to the next one, and some of them maintained religious and political animosities with a long history in Europe. Americans of radically different backgrounds and assumptions had been given no time to get used to each other; the nation's very identity was in flux, and in question. The USA was a work in progress. Every

Mencken biographer, attempting to deal fairly with his ethnocentric excesses, discovers what by modern standards is obsessive ethnic awareness. In his diary and memoirs, Mencken rarely mentions anyone without an ethnic footnote, often a condescending one.

Jews received the worst. Fred Hobson remarks that he seemed "fascinated" by them, an observation corroborated in *The American Language*, the least controversial or confrontational of his major works, where Mencken devotes a disproportionate five pages to Jewish surnames and the many Anglo-aping names Jews adopted in order to assimilate. Anecdotally they included, to Mencken's great delight, even such blueblood Boston names as Cabot and Lowell. For Mencken's detractors, this particular chapter is a windfall; it reads like a warning to college admissions officers and country-club membership committees—"Don't be fooled by surnames." There's a footnote, too, that fails to pass close political inspection: "Jewishness, on occasion, is a heavy burden, for there is always more or less anti-Semitism afloat. Its causes remain to be investigated. The reasons for it that Jews commonly accept are almost as dubious as those advanced by anti-Semites."

But of course no ethnic group was exempt from Mencken's disparagement. Those of us from the British Isles can find Anglo-Saxons described as "baboons," Scots "vulgar and lowdown . . . near the bottom of the civilized races." Poles were "a gang of brutal ignoramuses," Norwegians "uncouth yokels," and so forth, ad nauseam. As much as anything, Mencken was guilty of committing thoughts to paper that should have remained in his cerebral cortex, a sure mark of egotism and limited self-awareness. We can't say how typical his opinions may have been, 100 years ago, because no one else left us 5 to 10 million words of unguarded commentary. But the sheer exoticism of this ethnic mélange of his youth must account for Mencken's exaggerated awareness of national origins. Jews were unusually exotic since most American Jews, especially those from eastern Europe, were recent arrivals who had passed through Ellis Island in Mencken's lifetime. The disease of anti-Semitism, ancient and still epidemic, was rooted in the religious intolerance of many Christians, but that was never Mencken's problem. To our ears, these rude exchanges of "kike," "wop," and "mick" sound like a sophomoric competition of some kind, as if by reviling every other ethnic group Mencken thinks he's scoring points for the Germans. Yet even his fellow German Americans were "mainly ignoramuses" when he disagreed with them.

The heterogeneous, polyglot nature of the city that formed him is not an excuse for the unfortunate habits of thought that Mencken so often betrayed and belabored. But it was a reality that demands consideration when we judge him, a reality in dramatic contrast to a twenty-first-century America where an Anglo-Kenyan sits in the White House and the Supreme Court consists entirely of Catholics and Jews. Even in the mid-1950s when he died, this would have seemed like science fiction. Without pardoning Mencken, we can claim confidently that he was not a hater, not the sort of bigot who acts on his prejudices. As editor of *The American Mercury*, he published more work by women, blacks, and Jews than any of his contemporaries in the mainstream media. He committed himself financially to help a number of individual Jews escape from Germany, and he appealed to FDR (unsuccessfully, to no one's surprise) to relax immigration quotas on German Jews in the late Thirties, when Hitler's worst intentions became clear. In 1930 he met Emma Goldman in Paris, and the notorious Jewish communist impressed him so much that he sponsored—

again unsuccessfully—her petition for a visa to return briefly to the United States.

The best research won't even support the general assumption that Mencken was xenophobic, that he could be classified as a nativist because he treated so many people like unwelcome foreigners. He doesn't qualify as a nativist, it seems, because he never thought of himself as a native. One of the most powerfully revealing passages in Hobson's biography is an entry from Mencken's diary dated April 1943: "I believe, in truth, that immigration is always unwise—that is, when it is not enforced. I believe my chances in Germany would have been at least as good as they have been in America, and maybe a good deal better. I was born here and so were my father and mother, and I have spent all of my 62 years here, but I still find it impossible to fit myself into the accepted patterns of American life and thought. After all these years, I remain a foreigner."

Besides its valedictory tone—the legendary hypochondriac was beginning to say good-bye, though he had 13 more years to live—this unexpected confession appears to contain a bigger piece of the inner Mencken than anything else he committed to paper. For all his apparent complacency and self-confidence, there were times when he viewed himself as a lonely outsider, and a failed, rejected one as well. That self-image should have made him especially sympathetic to Jews, and perhaps it did, in the inverse, paradoxical way of all truths about the unfathomable Henry Mencken. There's an irreconcilable contradiction between the way he lived his life, in the affectionate company of so many Jews, and the gratuitously ugly things he wrote about them. It's almost as if he feared, at the Final Judgment, that he would be condemned as a Jew-lover, a *Judenfreund*, and stripped of his *lederhosen* by some racist Teutonic Almighty.

Turn-of-the-century America was a maelstrom of ethnic

confusion, which seems to have left young Mencken and others with a peculiar, unhealthy fixation on racial differences. To our ears it's uncouth, and bizarre. Yet imagine the satire Mencken might have made of the modern obsession with cell phones, which are rapidly becoming a part of the human body. If the language police of uncomprehending later generations have tarnished a reputation that was already fragile, it's not a decline that would have troubled H. L. Mencken. He despised anyone who pursued popularity or played to the cheap seats for encores. A greater pity is that his volcanic prose, such a soul-satisfying weapon of mass destruction when he trained it on proper targets, was so often wasted on what seem like petty, parochial differences today.

If he could return to see what posterity has made of his work, he would be highly amused to find himself demonized by the rigid Left and deified by the rigid Right—two equally slow-witted responses to that same ethnic chip Mencken always carried on his shoulder. The one posthumous disaster that might have pained him was the dismal fate of *The American Mercury*, his brainchild, which in its prime published some of the most sophisticated literature and criticism available to American readers. It was sold and "repositioned" many times, by progressively more conservative owners, and finally fell into the hands of neo-Nazis and white supremacists, denizens of what even the *National Review* could only describe as "the fever swamps of anti-Semitism." The *Mercury* endured, in various fascist costumes, until 1981. Mencken, never a convert to the secular faith of human progress, would have been appalled but not surprised.

Recessional

Henry Louis Mencken was the greatest American journalist of the last century and possibly the best writer of American English ever. He was also an asshole, and it is for the latter quality that we are doomed to remember him, if we remember him at all.

—Daniel Raeburn, *The Baffler*, 2003

THIS RECENT assessment, so generous on the high side and so unsparing on the low, concisely addresses two things— why it's a mistake to ignore Mencken, and why so many people choose to make that mistake. Though I've learned that attempts to channel him are largely futile, I tried to imagine whether Mencken himself would grin or snort in disgust if he could read this twenty-first-century précis of his life. I'm not sure. Mencken was free with coarse racial epithets and reputed to use anatomical Anglo-Saxonisms in casual speech—probably when he was torturing the squeamish Charles Angoff—but in his day no "civilized" literary gentleman would have committed that seven-letter word to print.

Manners change, even among those who make impoliteness their trademark. *The Baffler*, which has been described as "a punk literary journal," is an irreverent periodical founded by undergraduates and conceived in satire and contrarianism, much as *The Smart Set* and *The American Mercury* were conceived by Mencken and Nathan. Its editors and writers are far more legitimate descendants of the Sage of Baltimore than the sour old white men of the H. L. Mencken Club. Daniel

Raeburn, who wrote the *Baffler* essay when he was in his early thirties, is one of America's foremost authorities on comic books and graphic novels, a maverick critical voice once praised (?) by the *Austin Chronicle* as "a twisted lovechild of Hunter S. Thompson and Susan Sontag." Raeburn and the *The Baffler*'s founders belong to a generation of Americans so distant from Mencken's time and sphere of influence that they probably picture the old man in knee breeches, like Ben Franklin. Yet they're his rightful heirs, and he wouldn't disown them. *L'enfant terrible* is a literary fashion that never goes out of style.

It comforts me, in an age when mass media and social media seem to have drained most of the beauty and meaning from the American vulgate, to know that there are individuals who appreciate both graphic novels and the elegance of H. L. Mencken's English prose. It was his glamorous language that seduced me and hundreds like me, future critics and columnists, would-be *enfants*. Like Richard Wright, I could feel the electric current that runs through those warlike sentences, the current that was already humming when Mencken was 20 years old. When I disagreed with him, it was still like listening to music. When I agreed, it was like electroshock therapy.

Mencken had important things to teach a critic—never understate or equivocate, never backpedal or apologize, never use a flaccid word when a steroidal one will do. But there was no profit in trying to imitate the style he had self-synthesized from the eighteenth-century savants and the Baltimore streets; imitation was as fruitless as trying to paint like Van Gogh. No one taught him to write like that, of course. He was a genius. "The best writer of American English ever"? "Best," like "greatest," is a sprawling sort of word that's not easy to hammer into place. Of all our ambitious writers, the ones who held themselves to high standards, he is the most addictively readable. Possibly because he could write, filigreed diction and all, almost as fast as he could think.

To call Mencken the "greatest" journalist of the Typewriter Century is only to acknowledge his influence, which was prodigious. He was a truly transitional figure, the man who took the Enlightenment into the street, who introduced a much larger cross section of America to science, logic, and the idea, if not always the essence, of elevated taste in literature, music, theater, and painting. According to Mencken, the blueblood elite had these cultural crown jewels locked away in their ivory towers, and if we accept that history his own role is genuinely Promethean. He was the trickster who called their bluff and stole their fire. Imagine it's 1925 in Baltimore and a man on a streetcar is reading Goethe. The conductor asks him how he came upon such a book, and he almost certainly answers "Mencken." My grandfather, a small-town businessman trained as a lawyer, seemed to take it for granted that the author of *Prejudices* was the wisest man of his generation.

"Greatest," "best," and "wisest" H. L. Mencken would have accepted with modest grace, as no less than his due. But what about the A-word, the worse-than-ethnic epithet an irreverent (but not hostile) young critic so rudely attached to the famous Mr. Mencken, like a rusty soup can fastened to the old cat's tail? If the great man deserves it, it's not, in my opinion, because of his distasteful delight in now-verboten ethnic slang. In the best of all possible worlds, these superfluous distinctions between human beings would all disappear, along with the words to describe them. In the real world they persist, and the language police of one century are poorly equipped to judge the vocabulary of another. Context is everything, and the politically correct tend to be absolutists, blind to context, history, and shades of gray.

If his stupid words damn him, his glorious ones save him, and enough of that. There are more serious problems with H. L. Mencken. Though he often inspired loyalty, he did not reliably reciprocate it. The ever-loyal Knopf, he notes in his memoirs, "showed a certain amount of the obnoxious tactlessness of his race." Hamilton Owens, who worked closely with him for years at the *Sunpapers*, remembered Mencken as a man unequaled in generous efforts "to keep his friendships green." In his diaries Mencken remembered Owens as "a time-server with no more principle in him than a privy rat."

The playwright Ben Hecht was a virtual disciple who called HLM "the hero-mind of my youth" and "my alma mater." "No single American mind," Hecht wrote, "influenced existence in the Republic as much as he did." Mencken, for his part, recalls that Hecht's "congenital Jewishness began to dominate him" when Hitler invaded Poland, and that "there was always something cheap and flashy about him." Theodore Dreiser and Scott Fitzgerald, who had equally high praise for Mencken and valued his friendship, were dissected with the same chilly hauteur by the merciless Master. George Jean Nathan, at one time his best friend and always his defender, he indicted for a "typically Jewish inferiority complex." There's a taste of conscious betrayal in Mencken's disloyalty, as well as the swollen self-regard of a writer who needs to have the last word on everyone, and to write it down as well.

And there's worse. Every biographer, everyone who commits to a thorough reading of Mencken's work, concludes that he was deficient in empathy. This creates an irony when he claims, in *Notes on Democracy*, that one of the mob-man's fatal weaknesses is "his mere incapacity to project himself into the place of the other, his deficiency in imagination." Alistair Cooke, an admirer and anthologist of Mencken's work, couldn't help remarking that it reveals "a strain of cruelty." The critic Carl Van Doren, in a favorable review of one of Mencken's collections, remarked that what it "most conspicuously lacks . . . is the mood of pity."

I got a sense of this conspicuous hole in the giant's humanity when I read in *Minority Report* that he recommended—in spite of his contempt for judges and prosecutors—the execution of another 2,000 prisoners annually, an "immense improvement" for America in his opinion. He never hesitated to exult, without apology, in the deaths of his enemies. But my patience was exhausted by his account of an unpleasant dinner at James Branch Cabell's home in Richmond, "made horrible by the presence of his son Ballard."

"His features were coarse and repulsive, his speech was muddled and unintelligible and he walked with the shambling gait of a gorilla," Mencken writes of Cabell's only son, who apparently suffered from Down syndrome. "He insisted on following us about and pressing his simian attentions on us. . . . It was exactly like going into an animal cage." The passage reeks of cruelty. After reading it I faced the possibility that I had over-romanticized Mencken, and that I would never have qualified as one of his cronies or disciples.

There are plenty of witnesses for the defense. He is reliably reported to have been fond of his neighbors' children, to have been one of those popular old men who always has a smile and a piece of candy for every urchin on the block. He had an affectionate relationship with his pet turtles. Sara Mayfield, who saw no evil in her idol, remembers how he loved to present women and children with carefully chosen gifts—and hated to receive anything in return. Even the biographer Hobson, after leading us, wincing, through the story of Cabell's son, felt the need to remind us that Mencken provided financial support for his family and friends, conscientiously visited the sick, corresponded with prisoners, and sometimes petitioned for their parole.

This veil of paradox never lifts, but it fails to mask unpleasant possibilities, aspects of an outsized personality that anyone but Mencken would have gone to great pains to conceal. Instead he flaunted them, in volume after volume of opinion and autobiography. His personality influences his readers, whether we're impressed or appalled, because finally everything he wrote was intended to reveal Henry Mencken to the world. When he seems to be cutting his own throat unnecessarily, we have to ask ourselves whether he doesn't know he's alienating us, or, as I'm sure he would have insisted, that he doesn't care.

There's ample evidence to justify Daniel Raeburn's impolite epithet, to stamp that stinging A-word on H. L. Mencken's eternal passport. But that doesn't begin to erase the positive side of his ledger. In a world where the Word itself is diminished, where language languishes and there are a million loud voices but no strong ones, there are many reasons to honor Mencken's memory. In the *Saturday Evening Post* in 2008, Tait Trussell asked rhetorically "whether there ever will be another one quite as big, quite as brave, quite as mad as Mencken." And the chorus replied, "No, no, never."

According to the conservative Catholic journalist Joseph Bottum, "The magisterial critic has no role left in America, really." That he's correct is obvious, but it might take a critical volume on cultural decay and the mass media to complete his argument. Perhaps Mencken's claim to a dignified place in the literary pantheon is best articulated in his own voice, in this rare reflective, noncombative frame of mind:

If I have accomplished anything in this world, it is this: That I have made life measurably more bearable for the civilized minority in America. The individuals of this minority are often surrounded by dark, dense seas of morons and so they tend to become helpless. I have reason to believe that my books and other writings have given a little comfort to many such persons and even inspired some of them to revolt.

In France 200 years earlier, François-Marie Arouet, known as Voltaire, might well have indulged in the same modest boast. Like Mencken, Voltaire had not purged himself of a stubborn cultural anti-Semitism. He once wrote of the Jews, "They are all of them born with raging fanaticism in their hearts, just as the Bretons and the Germans are born with blond hair. I would not be in the least surprised if these people would not some day become deadly to the human race." Maybe we wouldn't have liked Voltaire much either. But that doesn't mean we should stop reading him. Or his brother bigot from Baltimore, who force-fed torpid America many of the Enlightenment's most indispensable ideas.

Acknowledgments

FOR THIS BOOK ON H. L. Mencken, who detested scholars, I am deeply indebted to three distinguished scholars. First, to Bob Richardson, who steered me and the book toward each other, and reassured me that it would be a fortunate collision. From crewing on his boat in the North Atlantic, I can testify that he has never yet steered me wrong. It's my hope that he won't find an anchorage misjudged here, or a starboard tack mishandled. Second, to Fred Hobson, not only for his superb biography that provided so much insight and signaled so many correct turns while I was researching HLM, but also for his encouragement and singular generosity over several decades, since we first realized that Mencken was an interest we shared. And third, to the late Louis Rubin Jr., who died while this book was in preparation. As a literary critic, newspaperman, and former resident of Baltimore, and as a Southerner born in 1923, Rubin often seemed, to those of us younger (but no longer young), like a direct link to Mencken and the era he dominated, back when men wore hats and smoked cigars indoors. Dr. Rubin measured Mencken as astutely as anyone who ever wrote or talked about him, and I'll never forget a long spring training game in Clearwater when our conversation covered most of H. L. Mencken and all the memorable World Series games of the 1930s.

My thanks also to Elisabeth Chretien, a remarkably patient and encouraging editor; to Mona Sinquefield, for her digital expertise that keeps me functioning—just barely—in the twenty-first century; to Redge Hanes, whose Uncle Fred and Aunt Betty were among Mencken's closest friends, for access to their correspondence; and once again, and always, to my wife, Lee Smith.

Bibliographic Essay

ANYONE WHO CLAIMS to have read every word H. L. Mencken published is a shameless liar; the percentage that I've read should qualify me, if less than an expert, as at least an earnest student of his work. My widest and most intense survey was accomplished a few years ago in a state of fear, when I was asked to deliver the annual lecture to the Mencken Society at the Enoch Pratt Free Library in Baltimore, and realized that my audience would be packed with Mencken scholars and biographers, as well as scores of lifelong enthusiasts, the kind who could tell you the cut and color of the great man's waistcoat at his high school graduation. (I committed only one factual error that I know of, but I was made aware of it.) For the purposes of this book I consulted a relatively small number of Mencken's published works, principally *My Life as Author and Editor* (Knopf, 1993); *The American Language* (Knopf, Abridged Edition, 1973); *Damn! A Book of Calumny* (Philip Goodman, 1918); *Treatise on the Gods* (Knopf, 1930); *Notes on Democracy* (Knopf, 1926); *Prejudices,* Series 1–6 (Knopf, 1919, 1920, 1922, 1924, 1926, 1927); *A Mencken Chrestomathy* (Knopf, 1949); *Happy Days* (Knopf, 1940); *Newspaper Days* (Knopf, 1941); *Heathen Days* (Knopf, 1943); *Minority Report: H. L. Mencken's Notebooks* (Knopf, 1956); and *The Letters of H. L. Mencken* (Knopf, 1961).

A reassuring presence atop this tower of Mencken's prose was my paperback copy of *The Vintage Mencken* (Vintage, 1956), the anthology selected by Alistair Cooke and presented to me by my grandfather when I was a teenager—my first taste of the addictive H. L. Mencken. I also found several very useful websites, the best a pair maintained by Richard Nordquist, who has collected some of the most interesting things Mencken wrote about language and the process of writing.

By far my greatest debt is to biographer Fred Hobson, author of *Mencken: A Life* (Random House, 1994). With a scholar's thoroughness and a journalist's eye and ear, with no ideological ax to grind, Hobson brings the elusive behemoth into sharper, more plausible focus than any of his previous or subsequent biographers. I have relied on Hobson's research and also, where there are troubling differences of opinion, on his judgment. The other writer who guided me most reliably through the smoky labyrinth of Mencken's pride and prejudice was the late (1923–2013) Louis D. Rubin Jr., critic, scholar, journalist, publisher, mentor to many of the South's most gifted writers and literary scholars. Any untested reader who conceives an appetite for Mencken would do well to begin with Hobson's book and with Rubin's essay "An Honorable Profession: H. L. Mencken of the Baltimore Sunpapers" (*Babe Ruth's Ghost*, University of Washington Press, 1996).

Among several biographies and memoirs that I sampled, the ones I found most useful were *The Constant Circle: H. L. Mencken and His Friends*, by Sara Mayfield (Delacorte, 1968), an unapologetically partisan but intriguing memoir from one of Sara Haardt Mencken's closest friends; *Mencken: The American Iconoclast*, by Marion Elizabeth Rodgers (Oxford University Press, 2005); and *The Skeptic: A Life of H. L. Mencken*, by Terry Teachout (HarperCollins, 2002). Always worthy of special mention is Charles Fecher's *Mencken: A Study of His Thought* (Knopf, 1978), which was invaluable to me when I was cramming for the Mencken lecture. For the uncollected letters of H. L. Mencken to Fred and Elizabeth Hanes, I am indebted to their nephew, the North Carolina writer and raconteur Redge Hanes.

Index

Adams, Henry, 26, 64
The American Language, 28, 52, 67, 81
The American Mercury, 6, 21, 51, 62, 68, 70, 71
Angoff, Charles, 8, 51, 62, 71
Arouet, François-Marie (Voltaire), 77
Aurelius, Marcus, 37

Babbitt, Irving, 42
Bierce, Ambrose, 12
Bloom, Marion, 38
A Book of Prefaces, 43, 47
Boston Brahmins, 10, 39, 64
Bottum, Joseph, 76
Boyd, Gerald, 30
Bryan, William Jennings, 10
Burke, Edmund, 58

Cabell, James Branch, 28, 35, 75
Céline, Louis-Ferdinand, 64
Chevalier, Maurice, 7
Clampett, Jed, 7
Clemens, Samuel, 18. *See also* Mark Twain
Conrad, Joseph, 11

Cooke, Alistair, 74, 82
Coolidge, Calvin, 36

Dawkins, Richard, 44
Dennis, C. J., 55
Douglas, Alfred (Lord), 64
Dreiser, Theodore, 4, 8, 28, 30, 42, 48, 64, 74
du Pont, Marcella, 35

Edison, Thomas, 54
Eliot, T. S., 4, 45, 64, 65
Emerson, Ralph Waldo, 38-39, 41, 45

Faulkner, William, 16
Fitzgerald, F. Scott, 28, 74
Ford, Ford Madox, 54
Foster, R. F., 66
"The Free Lance," 49

Goodman, Philip, 4, 65, 81

Hanes, Elizabeth (Betty), 7, 15, 35, 83
Harding, Warren G., 32
Hardy, Thomas, 54